AVOY PUBLISHING
· The Complete Estate & Property Planning Series ·
· Book 2 of 4 ·

PROBATE EXPLAINED

A Practical Guide to Settling Estates, Protecting Loved Ones, and Honoring Your Legacy

A. Perkins

AVOY PUBLISHING

First Edition · 2026

Probate Explained: A Practical Guide to Settling Estates, Protecting Loved Ones, and Honoring Your Legacy.

First Edition · 2026 · Printed in the United States of America.

Published in the United States of America by AVOY, LLC ('AVOY Publishing'). AVOY, LLC maintains the worldwide publication and distribution rights to this work.

Permissions and editorial inquiries may be directed to ap@avoyhq.com.

Print ISBN (Hardcover): 978-1-969048-82-1

Print ISBN (Paperback): 978-1-969048-81-4

eBook ISBN: 978-1-969048-83-8

Audiobook ISBN: 978-1-969048-84-5

Cover design and interior typography by AVOY, LLC. Typeset in Georgia and presented in the AVOY house style: burgundy and bronze on cream.

Publisher's Cataloging-in-Publication data available upon request.

For the families who learn the law

during the hardest week of their lives,

and for the lawyers who explain it patiently.

LEGAL NOTICE & DISCLAIMER

◆

This book is intended for general educational and informational purposes only. It does not constitute, and is not a substitute for, legal, tax, accounting, investment, insurance, or other professional advice. The law of probate, estate administration, and post-mortem property transfer is governed primarily by the individual states; statutes, court rules, judicial decisions, and tax authorities vary materially by jurisdiction and change over time. Application of any concept discussed in these pages to a particular set of facts requires individualized counsel from a qualified, licensed professional admitted to practice in the relevant jurisdiction.

Discussion of state-specific provisions — including the Uniform Probate Code and selected statutes of California, Florida, Texas, New York, Nevada, Pennsylvania, and Illinois — is offered at a conceptual and comparative level. Such discussion is neither exhaustive nor a substitute for the underlying statutes, which should be consulted directly together with current case law and court rules of the relevant probate court.

Names, fact patterns, and dialogue used in case studies, hypothetical examples, and “What This Looks Like in Practice” sections are illustrative composites. Any resemblance to actual persons, families, decedents, executors, administrators, or estates is coincidental and unintentional. No client-lawyer or advisor-client relationship is formed by reading this book or by following any example within it.

References to federal estate, gift, and generation-skipping transfer taxes are grounded in the Internal Revenue Code as in effect at the time of writing. Federal exemption amounts, rate schedules, and procedural requirements change. Readers should obtain current figures and current procedural guidance before acting.

Neither the author nor AVOY, LLC, nor any contributor, editor, or reviewer accepts liability for any loss or damage caused, directly or indirectly, by reliance on the contents of this book. Readers are urged to obtain individualized professional advice before opening, administering, contesting, settling, closing, or otherwise relying upon any matter of probate or estate administration.

By continuing to read this book, the reader acknowledges and accepts the terms of this notice.

CONTENTS

A LETTER FROM THE PUBLISHER

◆

If you have opened this book, you are almost certainly one of two kinds of reader.

You may be someone who has just lost a parent, a spouse, a sibling, or a close friend, and you have been told — by a lawyer, by a bank teller, by an older relative who has been through this once before — that the estate now needs to "go through probate." You have a folder of papers in front of you. You have a list of accounts you cannot access. You have a will whose meaning is no longer obvious, or no will at all. You are tired, you are grieving, and you are being asked to make decisions on a clock you did not set.

Or you may be someone who has not yet lost anyone, but who has begun to wonder, quietly, what will happen to the people you love when you are gone. You have heard the word probate used as a warning. You have read articles that describe it as a process to be avoided at all costs. You suspect the truth is more complicated, and you would like, just once, for someone to explain the thing without trying to sell you anything.

This book is for both of you.

Probate Explained is a volume in AVOY Publishing's Legacy Series. It is not a sales pitch for a particular trust company, a particular law firm, or a particular jurisdiction. It is a book about one of the most widely misunderstood institutions in American private law: the probate court and the process of estate administration that runs through it.

The book takes a position. It says that probate is neither the catastrophe the marketing literature suggests nor the simple paperwork the courthouse clerk implies. It is a structured legal procedure with a specific function, a predictable sequence, and a small set of pressure points where ordinary families consistently get into trouble. Once you understand the structure, the ground stops shifting under your feet. The fear, in most cases, drops away.

"Probate is not the punishment that happens to a family. It is the system that transfers ownership when the previous owner is no longer here to do it."

We have written it on the assumption that you are an intelligent adult who has been talked down to enough times by people in suits. Where the law is technical, we say so. Where it is not, we use ordinary words. Where the outcome depends on a state-by-state distinction, we point that out and tell you which states fall on which side of the line.

We have also written it on the assumption that you may have a will, a trust, both, or neither — and that the path through probate is meaningfully different in each of those four worlds. We will treat all four. We will not pretend that one is universally better than another. The right answer, in private law, is almost always: it depends on the specific structure you actually have.

Particular care has been taken with the moments when families typically stumble: the first thirty days after death, the appointment of the personal representative, the creditor-claim window, the inventory and appraisal, the petition for distribution, and the closing of the estate. Each of those moments has its own logic. Each has its own way of producing avoidable conflict. We will spend time on all of them.

We are not your lawyer. The Legal Notice on the previous page is not ceremonial. Probate sits at the intersection of fifty state systems, federal tax law, court rules that change without notice, and the lived realities of a family in grief. A book can show you the architecture. It cannot draft your particular petition. When you act on something in these pages, do it with the help of qualified counsel in the relevant jurisdiction.

With that, we offer you the volume.

— AVOY Publishing

Spring 2026

HOW TO READ THIS BOOK

◆

The book is organized in six movements.

You can read them in order, the way they were written, and you will end up with a complete mental model of probate: what it is, when it happens, who runs it, why it takes the time it takes, where families get stuck, and how it ends. By the time you reach the Conclusion you will know more about probate than 95 percent of the population — including most adult children and most spouses who arrive at the courthouse for the first time.

Or you can read whichever Part answers the question you came with. Each chapter stands alone. The cross-references will get you back to anything you skipped.

A few suggestions, depending on who you are.

If you have just lost someone.
Read Chapter 3 first. It treats the first thirty days after death and explains, calmly, why nothing seems to be happening yet. Then read Chapter 4 (the Executor's role) and Chapter 5 (what the court does). Those three chapters together will tell you what to expect for the next several months.

If you have been named in a will as executor and you do not know what that means.

Read Chapter 4 carefully, then Appendix C (the Executor's First-Sixty-Days Checklist) and Appendix G (the Twelve-Month Estate Administration Calendar). These three documents together cover roughly ninety percent of what your role actually requires.

If you are trying to understand whether your own affairs would go through probate.

Read Chapter 2 first. It explains exactly which assets require probate and which transfer outside it. Then read Chapter 8 on the misunderstandings that produce the most surprises in this area.

If you have an attorney and you want to walk into the next meeting informed.

Read Chapter 7 (delays and disputes), Appendix A (Glossary), and Appendix D (common forms and what they mean). You will leave that meeting with a structure you actually understand, not a binder you do not.

A note on the prose. Where the book uses a technical term — letters testamentary, pour-over will, ancillary probate, residuary estate — the term is defined the first time it appears, and re-defined any time it shows up in a chapter where the reader may have lost the thread. Where the law is truly complicated, we say so and slow down. Where it is not, we move quickly. The Glossary in the back catches anything that drifts.

A Note on the Reading Conventions

Three small visual conventions appear throughout the book. They are easy to recognize and worth understanding before you begin.

Chapter at a Glance

Every chapter opens with a short bullet list under the heading "Chapter at a Glance." It tells you what the chapter is about and what you will know by the end. Read it as a map. Skip it if you would rather discover the territory as you go.

KEY POINT callouts

Boxed in burgundy with a "KEY POINT" label, these are the most important structural facts in each chapter — the sentences that, if you remembered nothing else from a given chapter, would still leave you better informed than ninety percent of readers approaching the subject for the first time. If you are skim-reading, read the KEY POINT boxes.

REFLECTION callouts

Boxed in bronze with a "REFLECTION" label, these are quieter notes — observations about how the procedure intersects with families, with grief, or with the deeper question of what probate is asking you to accept. They are not summaries. They are pauses. Skip them if you are reading in a hurry; return to them later when the work is closer.

WHAT IS PROBATE? definition box

Boxed in steel-blue and labeled “WHAT IS PROBATE?”, this single callout appears in the Preface and supplies the working definition of probate that the rest of the book builds on. If you read nothing else before Chapter 1, read that box.

What This Looks Like in Practice

Most chapters include a short narrative vignette under this heading. The vignettes are illustrative composites — names and details are invented, but the patterns they describe are common in probate practice. They are intended to ground the abstract architecture of the chapter in the texture of a real family's experience.

Tables, Figures, and the Glossary

Tables are labeled “Table X.X” and figures are labeled “Figure X.X.” They are integrated into the text where they help, never as decoration. The Glossary in the back of the book defines every technical term used in the chapters; if a word stops you, the Glossary will start you again.

What's at the Back of This Book

Roughly the back third of this volume is reference material. It is meant to be returned to long after the first reading, when the work is no longer abstract. We list it here so you know what is waiting for you when you need it.

- **Conclusion.** The philosophical close — what the institution of probate is for, in plain language.
- **Reader FAQ.** Twenty-six common questions, organized by category — Estates & Trusts, Living Wills & Advance Directives, and Health & Medical Law — with every answer cross-referenced to the chapter that treats it in full.
- **Glossary of Probate Terms.** Forty-four entries. Every technical word in the book, defined in plain English, with chapter cross-references.
- **Bibliography & Reference Guide.** Statutory sources, treatises, practitioner guides, periodicals, and online resources for the reader who wants to dig deeper.
- **About the Publisher and About the Author.** AVOY Publishing's mission and the author's background.
- **Fourteen Appendices (A–N).** Probate at a Glance · Small-Estate Procedures by State · Executor's First-Sixty-Days Checklist · Common Probate Forms and What They Mean · Sample Letter of Instruction · Annotated Reading List · Twelve-Month Estate Administration Calendar · Family Communication Framework · Subject Index · Reader's Quick-Start Guide · Notes on The Complete Estate & Property Planning Series · Chapter-by-Chapter Summary · Creditor-Claim Priority Order · Ancillary Probate.

Together the back matter is a compact reference library. If you came to the book in crisis, the Reader's Quick-Start Guide (Appendix J) and the First-Sixty-Days Checklist (Appendix C) will be the most useful pages you read this week.

Begin where it serves you. Return as your circumstances change. The book is designed for both first reading and tenth.

A NOTE ON THE MAKING OF THIS VOLUME

◆

A book like this could be written in two ways.

It could be written by a probate lawyer, in the language probate lawyers use, with a footnote on every other page and a chapter on the rule against perpetuities that nobody finishes. Several such books exist. They are useful to lawyers.

Or it could be written by someone who has watched probate unfold from the other side of the bench — who has sat with families during the first week, watched executors learn what authority they actually have and do not have, watched simple estates close in eight months and complicated ones drift into their second and third year, and listened to the same misunderstandings repeat themselves across a hundred different families. That is the perspective from which this book is written.

The author is not a probate lawyer and does not pretend to be one. He is, however, someone who has spent more than a decade observing private estate administration in close proximity — as an executor, as a beneficiary, as a settlor of trusts that interact with probate, and as the person whom families in his orbit have turned to when they did not know who else to ask. The result is a book that takes the law seriously without pretending to be the law itself.

Where the text describes a state statute or a procedural rule, the description is grounded in the rule as it stood at the time of writing. Where the text describes how probate performs in real life, the description is grounded in observation of how probate has performed for real families over the past decade and longer.

This is, in short, a practitioner's book — written for readers who would rather understand the architecture than be sold a brochure of it.

PREFACE

◆

The first thing to know about probate is that it is older than almost everything else you are likely to compare it to.

Older than the modern corporation. Older than the income tax. Older than the United States. Older than the common law of England that produced it. Older than the printing press that distributed the cases that shaped it.

> **WHAT IS PROBATE?**
>
> The probate idea — that when someone dies, a neutral authority must confirm the will, gather the property, pay the debts, and hand what remains to the rightful heirs — is older than two thousand years.

Roman law had a version of it. Medieval ecclesiastical courts in England ran a version of it for the better part of a millennium. American probate courts inherited the framework, modified it for a federal system of fifty independent states, and have spent the past three centuries refining the procedure case by case.

The institution has survived, in one form or another, because it solves a problem no other institution solves quite as cleanly: at the moment of death, property still exists, but the owner is gone. Banks will not release funds to someone who claims to be the heir. Title to a house cannot be re-recorded on the basis of a phone call. Creditors cannot be told to wait indefinitely. Someone, somewhere, has to be given the legal authority to act for an estate whose owner is no longer present to act for it.

Probate is the system that creates that authority.

We will move through it in stages. We will begin with what probate is and why it exists. We will move into the question of when probate is necessary and when it is not, because that question — more than any other — drives the experience a particular family will have. We will spend the middle of the book on the personal representative, on the court, and on the calendar — the three forces that, together, shape every probate administration. We will turn in Part IV to the places where families consistently get stuck, and in Part V to the moments when the process becomes deeply, unavoidably personal. We will close in Part VI with the question of how probate ends — quietly, without ceremony, and with a transfer of ownership that often goes unnoticed by the people who benefit from it.

Read with patience. The subject rewards it.

INTRODUCTION

Why This Book Exists

Most people encounter probate at the worst possible moment.

Someone has just died. Emotions are high. Information is fragmented. Family members are asking questions no one knows how to answer. And suddenly there is a court involved in what feels like a deeply private matter.

Probate feels intrusive, slow, and intimidating not because it is designed to be cruel, but because it is poorly understood. The system was designed by people who were not in a hurry, for a problem in which haste produces fraud, and it operates on a calendar that almost never matches the calendar of grief. The mismatch is the source of nearly every complaint families ever raise about probate. The mismatch is also the system working as intended.

This book exists for one reason: to explain what probate actually is, what it does, and what happens next — without fear, without salesmanship, and without pretending it is something it is not.

Probate is not punishment.

It is not a trap.

It is not always avoidable.

It is a legal process with a specific function, a predictable sequence, and a small set of clear points where families get confused.

Once you understand the structure, much of the anxiety drops away.

Every year, a very large number of American families lose a meaningful share of their inheritance to four things they could have planned for and did not.

The first is delay — months and sometimes years lost to procedural waiting periods, missing documents, and uncontested matters that simply could not be advanced because no one had the authority to advance them.

The second is friction — fees, costs, accounting bills, and the small frictional taxes that probate administration imposes on every estate even when no one is fighting.

The third is conflict — disputes among heirs that probate did not cause but that the structure of probate often makes both visible and durable.

The fourth is privacy — the loss of confidentiality that comes from the fact that probate is, by design and almost everywhere in the United States, a public proceeding. Wills are filed. Inventories are filed. Creditors are notified. The community learns what the family had. For some families that is fine. For others it is precisely what they did not want.

Each of these four costs can be planned for. Some can be avoided entirely with the right structure put in place during life. Most can be sharply reduced even after the structure is already set.

This book exists because most of what is written about probate is written either for lawyers — and is therefore unreadable to anyone else — or for marketing purposes, and is therefore not telling the whole truth. The space in the middle — a book that respects the reader's intelligence, defines its terms, takes the law seriously, names what probate can and cannot do, and tells the truth about the practical experience of running an estate — has been mostly empty.

We wrote this volume to fill it.

By the time you finish, you will know:

- What probate actually is, structurally, in plain English.
- Which assets pass through probate and which transfer automatically outside of it.
- What the first thirty days after a death typically look like, and why so little appears to happen during them.
- What an executor or personal representative is, what authority that role carries, and what it does not.
- What the probate court actually does — and the much larger set of things it does not.

- Why probate takes the time it takes, and which parts of the calendar are immovable.
- Where probate cases get stuck — the small handful of issues that account for most delay and most dispute.
- What families consistently get wrong about probate, and how those misunderstandings become avoidable conflict.
- Why the process feels so personal even when nothing about it is meant to be.
- How probate ends, and what the closing of an estate looks like in practice.

This is not legal advice. It is a foundation. With it, you will be in a position to ask better questions, evaluate better answers, and make better decisions about a process that arrives, sooner or later, in nearly every American family.

That is the value of a book like this.

Let us begin.

PART I

◆

FOUNDATIONS

What probate is, why it exists, and when it touches an estate.

CHAPTER 1

What Probate Is (and Why It Exists)

Chapter at a Glance

- What probate is, defined in one sentence — and why that sentence creates so much misunderstanding.
- Why probate exists at all — the structural problem at death that no other institution solves cleanly.
- The probate court as a court of paperwork rather than a court of grievances.
- The three things probate actually does, in this exact order: authority, notice and claims, distribution.
- Why the procedure varies by state — and why that variation matters more than most readers expect.

Probate is the legal process by which a court oversees the transfer of a person's assets after death.

That sentence alone causes tension. The word court suggests conflict. The word oversees suggests loss of control. The idea that property must pass through a formal process feels unnecessary, especially when a will exists. Most adults assume

— reasonably enough — that the will itself is the instruction set, and that following it ought to be a private matter for the family. They are surprised to discover that it is not.

Probate exists because, at the moment of death, an immediate legal problem arises: property is still owned, but the owner no longer exists. Title to a house is in a name attached to a person who is no longer here. A bank account sits frozen in a name no one is now authorized to use. A retirement account with a beneficiary designation can pay out, but a brokerage account in a single name cannot. A car has a title. The car still exists. The owner does not.

Someone, somewhere, has to be given the legal authority to:

- identify and collect the deceased person's assets,
- evaluate and pay valid debts,
- resolve outstanding claims,
- transfer remaining ownership lawfully to the people entitled to it.

Probate is the system that creates that authority. Without it, there would be no neutral mechanism to prevent fraud, protect creditors, resolve disputes, or confirm who has the right to act on behalf of someone who can no longer act for themselves.

Probate, in other words, is not about families. It is about title and authority. The family is involved only because property law is involved, and the family is who the property is supposed to reach.

A Court of Limited Purpose

The probate court is not a court of grievances. It is a court of paperwork. Its institutional purpose is narrow and procedural: to confirm that a person has died, to identify the document (if any) that purports to be their last will, to appoint a personal representative empowered to administer the estate, to oversee the orderly satisfaction of debts and claims, and to approve the final transfer of property to the rightful heirs or beneficiaries.

It is not a forum for emotional reckoning. It is not a forum for family reconciliation. It is not a forum for evaluating whether the deceased was a good or bad parent, partner, or friend. The court has no interest in those questions and no jurisdiction over them. Its single sustained question is narrower than that: did this estate's administrator follow the law, discharge the recognized duties, and account properly for what came in and what went out. Every other question the family may have is, from the court's perspective, beside the point.

> **KEY POINT**
>
> Probate is not about families. It is about title, authority, and the orderly satisfaction of legal claims against the estate of a person who is no longer here to satisfy them themselves.

The Three Things Probate Actually Does

Strip the procedure to its essentials and probate does three things, in this order:

1. **Authority.** It identifies a single, accountable person — the executor named in a will, or in the absence of a will, an administrator chosen by statutory priority — and gives that person formal court-issued authority to act for the estate. That document is called Letters Testamentary (when there is a will) or Letters of Administration (when there is not). Without those Letters, no bank, no brokerage, no county recorder, and no insurance company will speak to anyone about the deceased's property.

2. **Notice and claims.** It opens a publicly noticed window — typically several months long — during which any creditor who believes they are owed money by the estate must come forward and present a claim, supported by evidence. Claims that are not presented in the window are time-barred. This part of probate is harsh by design: its function is to give the estate finality. A family that closes a probate without leaving a creditor window open behind them is not at meaningful risk of a creditor appearing five years later.

3. **Distribution.** After valid debts and claims are paid, taxes are filed, and the court is satisfied that the personal representative has discharged their duties, the court

authorizes the transfer of remaining property to the people legally entitled to it. The will, if there is one, says who. State law of intestate succession says who if there is not.

Almost every fact about a particular probate case can be traced back to one of those three functions. When something seems strange — a bank refusing to act, a creditor surfacing late, an heir threatening to sue — it is almost always because the case is in or moving between those three phases.

Where the Authority Comes From

The probate court's authority is statutory. Each state has a probate code (in some states the Probate Code, in others the Surrogate's Court Procedure Act, the Estates and Trusts Code, or the Uniform Probate Code as enacted in that state) that defines, in detail, what the court can do, who has standing to appear, what notice is required, and how distribution is approved. The judge sitting in a probate matter is not exercising broad equitable authority. The judge is applying a statute. Most of what looks discretionary is, in fact, the application of a procedural rule that allows a single answer.

This is why two probate cases in two different states can produce sharply different timelines, different cost profiles, and different levels of intrusiveness — even when the underlying family situation is identical. The statute differs. The court rules differ. The local culture of probate practice differs. What is routine and quiet in one state can be slow and public in another. We will return to this in Chapter 6.

Probate Is Not Failure

It is worth saying directly, because it is so widely assumed otherwise: the fact that an estate goes through probate does not mean the deceased did anything wrong.

Probate happens to estates whose owners had wills, and to estates whose owners did not. It happens to estates with carefully drawn estate plans, and to estates with no plan at all. It happens because of how a particular asset was titled — an account left in a single name, a deed not yet retitled into a trust, an old life insurance policy whose beneficiary was never updated. Most probate cases do not arise from neglect. They arise from how ordinary lives accumulate property, and how easy it is, in the press of daily life, to leave one or two things untitled.

Conversely, the fact that an estate avoided probate does not mean the deceased was unusually wise. It usually means a trust was funded properly, a small handful of accounts had beneficiary designations, and joint titling with right of survivorship covered the rest. None of those mechanisms is secret. None of them requires special wealth. What they require is a small amount of attention paid before death — attention that the system rewards but does not insist on.

Where We Go From Here

What This Looks Like in Practice

Consider the family of a long-time small-business owner — call him Robert — who has just died at seventy-two after a brief illness. He left a four-page will, dated nine years before his death, naming his wife as primary beneficiary and his two adult children as contingent beneficiaries. The will named one of his children, an accountant, as executor. He owned a house jointly with his wife, two cars in his individual name, an IRA with his wife as named beneficiary, a brokerage account in his individual name, and a forty-percent ownership interest in a small construction company he had run for thirty years.

On day three, Robert's wife and adult children sit in his accountant-child's living room and try to make sense of what happens next. They have heard the word probate. They are not sure what it means. The wife wonders, fairly, why she cannot simply continue paying the bills as she always has. The accountant-child suspects the answer is more complicated than that and calls the family's longtime estate-planning lawyer.

What that lawyer tells them, over the next two hours, is the entire subject of this book. Some of Robert's property will move outside probate without any court involvement at all. Some will need a court-appointed personal representative to act for it. Some — the construction company — will require careful valuation and possibly negotiation with the deceased's business partners. Some — the IRA — will pay out by beneficiary designation in a few weeks regardless of what probate is doing. And some — the brokerage account, the cars, and Robert's interest in the company — will require Letters Testamentary, an inventory, a creditor-claim window, and a court-approved final accounting before they can move.

By the end of that conversation, what had felt like an undifferentiated catastrophe begins to organize itself into a manageable list. The family does not yet feel calm. But they have stopped feeling lost. That is what understanding the architecture does, and that is the work this book sets out to do for every reader who arrives at it.

The rest of Part I lays the groundwork. Chapter 2 explains exactly which kinds of assets require probate and which transfer automatically outside it; if there is one chapter most readers will return to, it is that one. Part II treats the opening months — the first thirty days after a death and the role of the personal representative — because nearly every reader who arrives at this book is somewhere inside that first calendar quarter. Part III addresses the court and the calendar. Part IV treats delay and dispute. Part V treats the human side of probate. Part VI treats the ending — the closing of an estate and the transfer of legacy.

Common Questions, Briefly

Two questions readers regularly raise after reading this chapter are worth treating directly here, before we move on.

Is probate the same as estate planning?

No. Estate planning is the work done during life to organize what happens at death — wills, trusts, beneficiary designations, powers of attorney, advance directives. Probate is the court process that operates after death on whatever estate plan (or absence of plan) the deceased left behind. A good estate plan shapes probate, narrows it, sometimes eliminates it. The two are related but distinct, and confusing them is one of the most common entry-level errors in this entire field.

Can I keep my own family out of probate court entirely?

Often, yes — but the answer depends on attention paid during life, not at death. The instruments that move property outside probate (revocable trusts, joint titling, beneficiary designations, transfer-on-death deeds) all require deliberate set-up. Done well, they can collapse a probate proceeding to essentially nothing. Done poorly, they leave gaps the probate court ends up filling. We treat this in detail in Chapter 2 and again in Chapter 8.

The book is long because the subject is layered. Read the parts you need.

Figure 1.1

The three things probate actually does, in this exact order.

KEY POINT

Probate is the legal mechanism for creating authority to act on behalf of property whose owner is no longer here. It is a court-supervised procedure whose three core functions — authority, notice and claims, distribution — together explain almost everything that ever happens in a probate case.

What This Chapter Has Said

Probate is not a moral judgment. It is not a sign that the deceased did anything wrong. It is the institutional response to a recurring legal problem: at death, property still exists, but the owner is gone. Someone must be given authority to act, creditors must be allowed to come forward, and remaining property must be transferred. The probate court is the institution that creates that authority and supervises its exercise. Its scope is narrow. Its calendar is structured. Its outcomes, in most cases, are predictable.

CHAPTER 2

When Probate Happens — and When It Doesn't

Chapter at a Glance

- The single test that determines whether probate is required: how the asset is titled at death.
- The two universes of property — probate and non-probate — and how to recognize each.
- Why a properly funded trust avoids most probate and why even a fully funded plan rarely avoids it entirely.
- Small-estate procedures: what they are, how the threshold works, and why the number changes over time.
- Three small structural failures that account for most surprise probate proceedings.

Probate does not happen automatically. It happens when assets require court involvement to change ownership. That is the entire test.

Two adults can die with identical net worth — say, two million dollars in houses, accounts, and personal property — and one estate can close in a courthouse-free, six-week administrative process, while the other estate drags through eighteen months of probate. The difference is not the size of the estate. The difference is how the assets were titled.

Two Kinds of Property at Death

At the moment of death, every piece of property the deceased owned falls into one of two categories:

1. Probate property — assets owned individually, in the deceased's name alone, with no automatic transfer mechanism attached.

2. Non-probate property — assets that, by their structure, transfer automatically by operation of law or by contract at the moment of death.

Probate is triggered when probate property exists. The size of the probate estate is the sum of those assets. Non-probate property never goes through the courthouse at all — not because anyone hid it, but because it does not need to.

Table 2.1

Asset	Default treatment	Why
House titled in deceased's name alone	Probate	No co-owner, no transfer-on-death deed, no trust ownership.
House titled jointly with right of survivorship	Non-probate	Survivor takes by operation of law.
House owned by a funded revocable trust	Non-probate	Trust owns the property; trustee continues administration.
Bank account in deceased's name alone	Probate	Bank requires Letters before releasing funds.
Bank account with POD beneficiary	Non-probate	Beneficiary presents death certificate; account transfers.
Brokerage account, single name, no TOD	Probate	Standard taxable account with no beneficiary mechanism.
Brokerage account with TOD designation	Non-probate	Transfer-on-death registration controls.
IRA / 401(k) with named beneficiary	Non-probate	Contract between custodian and beneficiary.
IRA / 401(k) with no living beneficiary	Probate	Default reverts to the estate.
Life insurance with named beneficiary	Non-probate	Insurance contract controls.
Life insurance payable to estate	Probate	Proceeds become a probate asset.
Vehicles in deceased's sole name	Probate (often)	Many states require Letters; a few allow expedited transfer.
Personal effects, household goods	Probate	Tangible personal property not separately retitled.
Business interests in sole name	Probate	Unless held by a trust or covered by a buy-sell agreement.

Asset	Default treatment	Why
Property held by a Lady-Bird or TOD deed	Non-probate	Death triggers automatic transfer of recorded interest.

Probate property versus non-probate property — typical examples.

Several patterns emerge from Table 2.1, and they are worth noticing.

First, probate is largely a function of titling. The same house can be a probate asset or a non-probate asset depending on whose name is on the deed and how that ownership is structured. Nothing about the house itself determines its treatment.

Second, contractual transfer mechanisms — payable-on-death beneficiary designations, transfer-on-death registrations, joint-with-right-of-survivorship titling — sit outside the probate system entirely. They are treated as part of a contract between the deceased and the financial institution. The court is not involved.

Third, the trust is the most powerful non-probate device because it is general-purpose. Where joint titling and beneficiary designations work for specific assets one at a time, a properly funded revocable trust can hold any asset and pass it outside probate. We treat the relationship between trusts and probate at length in the companion volume Trust Made Simple.

What Triggers Probate

Probate is triggered when, at death, there is at least one probate asset of meaningful value still in the deceased's individual name.

What counts as meaningful value depends on the state. Most states have a small-estate threshold — a dollar amount under which a simplified administrative procedure replaces full probate. Below that threshold, a small-estate affidavit (or its state equivalent) lets a successor collect the property without opening a formal estate. The threshold varies considerably:

Table 2.2

State	Approximate threshold	Procedure
California	$184,500 (gross, real and personal)	Small Estate Affidavit; Spousal Property Petition for marital assets.
Florida	$75,000 (probate assets)	Summary Administration available; Disposition Without Administration for very small estates.
Texas	$75,000 (excluding homestead and exempt property)	Affidavit of Heirship; Small Estate Affidavit.
New York	$50,000 (personal property)	Voluntary Administration in Surrogate's Court.
Illinois	$100,000 (personal property)	Small Estate Affidavit.
Pennsylvania	$50,000 (personal property)	Petition for Settlement of Small Estate.
Nevada	$25,000 (no real property) / $100,000 (with court order)	Affidavit of Entitlement; Set-Aside Petition.
Ohio	$45,000 (with surviving spouse) / $5,000 (without)	Release from Administration.

Selected small-estate thresholds (figures change; verify with current state law).

These figures move. The state legislatures revise them every few years, usually upward, to reflect inflation and to expand the population of estates that can avoid full probate. The current number for any state is a phone call to the probate court clerk away. The point of Table 2.2 is not the precise dollar amount but the structural pattern: every state recognizes that small estates do not need full probate and creates a faster lane for them.

Three Common Probate Triggers

Even with thoughtful planning, probate is often triggered by one of three small structural failures:

(1) An asset never made it into the trust. The trust agreement was signed. The trust was funded with the brokerage account, the bank accounts, and the primary house. Then the deceased bought a vacation property four years later and never transferred title into the trust. The vacation property is a probate asset. Everything else is not. The estate goes through a probate procedure for that one asset alone — a smaller and faster proceeding than a full estate, but a court proceeding all the same.

(2) A beneficiary designation was never updated. A retirement account has the deceased's first spouse listed as beneficiary, even though the deceased remarried fifteen years ago. The first spouse is alive. The contract controls. The current spouse may have a claim under state law against the estate, which is a probate matter. The retirement account itself, however, pays out per the beneficiary designation. We will return to the consequences of stale beneficiary designations in Chapter 7.

(3) A joint owner predeceased. A house was titled jointly between two siblings with right of survivorship. One sibling died first. The surviving sibling did not retitle. When the surviving sibling later dies, the house is in their individual name

alone — and is therefore a probate asset of the second-to-die estate. Joint titling provides survivorship between the originally named co-owners; it does not extend to the survivors of the survivor.

When Probate Is Required Even With a Trust

It surprises many readers that an estate with a fully funded living trust may still require a small probate proceeding. The most common reasons:

- An asset acquired late in life and never funded into the trust.
- A pour-over will whose only function is to direct any forgotten asset into the trust at death — the will itself must be admitted to probate even though the trust controls disposition.
- Tort claims that survive the deceased (a wrongful-death cause of action, an outstanding personal-injury claim) — these are typically probate-administered even when the rest of the estate is not.
- An ancillary probate in another state, where the deceased owned real property in a state different from their state of residence.

> **REFLECTION**
>
> A trust does not eliminate the possibility of probate. It reduces the surface area where probate can attach, often to nearly zero. "Nearly" is not "none." The careful estate plan anticipates the small remainder and treats it as routine, not as failure.

Probate Is About Structure, Not About Wealth

What This Looks Like in Practice

Two siblings — call them Anne and Marcus — each lose a parent in the same calendar year. The two estates are nearly identical in net worth, around two million dollars apiece, accumulated over forty years of careful saving. The two estates have entirely different experiences.

Anne's mother had set up a revocable living trust eight years before her death. The trust held the house, the brokerage accounts, and the ownership of a small rental duplex. Bank accounts were retitled into the trust at the same time. The retirement account had a current beneficiary designation. The car titles were re-registered in the trust's name. When Anne's mother died, the successor trustee — Anne — took over administration the next morning. There was no court appearance. There was no Letters Testamentary. The estate had a small probate proceeding to admit the pour-over will (no assets fell out of the trust during her last year), but the entire matter was wrapped up administratively in three months.

Marcus's father had a will. The will was well-drafted. It named Marcus as executor and left the estate equally to Marcus and his two siblings. The father's house was in his individual name. His brokerage account was in his individual name. His bank account was in his individual name. His retirement account had named beneficiaries. When Marcus's father died, the will controlled the non-retirement assets, and a full probate proceeding was required to administer them. Letters Testamentary issued in week eight. The creditor-claim window ran through month seven. The estate closed in month thirteen, a typical timeline for an uncontested estate of moderate complexity.

Neither family did anything wrong. Their parents' choices about asset titling — made years before either parent died — produced the entire difference in experience. Anne's mother had spent an afternoon in a lawyer's office eight years earlier and had then spent another afternoon over the next year retitling the assets. That single sequence of small decisions saved Anne approximately fourteen months of administration.

We will end this chapter where we began it. Probate is not a function of how much money exists. It is a function of how ownership was structured before death. Two estates with the same balance sheet can have entirely different probate experiences. The variable is not wealth. The variable is titling, and beneficiary designations, and the presence or absence of a funded trust. Those choices are made — or not made — long before the deceased ever thought they mattered.

Notes on Practice

Several practical patterns show up so consistently in probate practice that they deserve a brief notice here.

The first pattern: the most common asset to be left out of a trust is a vehicle. Cars are bought, registered, paid off, and sold over a lifetime, and most people never think to retitle them into the trust between purchases. By the time of death the car often sits as an individual-name probate asset that would not have been there if the buyer had simply asked the DMV for the trust-titling option at registration.

The second pattern: the most common asset to have a stale beneficiary designation is the deceased's first job's 401(k). It was set up at age twenty-five, with a parent or sibling as beneficiary, and was never updated through marriage, remarriage, or the birth of children. Most plan administrators now require periodic re-acknowledgment of beneficiary designations precisely to address this — but the legacy problem remains widespread.

The third pattern: the most common asset misclassified as non-probate is a bank account where the deceased intended a TOD designation but never completed the bank's form. Verbal promise to a child does not create a TOD. The bank's form, signed and dated, does. Without the form, the account is a probate asset regardless of the deceased's intent.

The next chapter takes up the question that follows: when probate is in fact triggered, what does the first thirty days actually look like.

Figure 2.1

PROBATE PROPERTY
Goes through court

- House in sole name
- Brokerage account, no TOD
- Bank account, no POD
- Vehicles in sole name
- Personal effects
- Business interest, sole name

NON-PROBATE PROPERTY
Transfers automatically

- Joint with right of survivorship
- Account with POD/TOD
- Retirement w/ named beneficiary
- Life insurance w/ beneficiary
- Property held by funded trust
- Lady-Bird / TOD deeds

The two universes of property at death — by titling, not by wealth.

KEY POINT

Probate is triggered by titling, not by wealth. The same balance sheet can produce a six-week administrative transfer or an eighteen-month formal probate, depending entirely on choices made about asset structure during life.

What This Chapter Has Said

Two universes of property exist at death: probate property, which moves only through the court process, and non-probate property, which transfers automatically by titling, contract, or trust ownership. The trigger for probate is the existence of individually titled assets at death. Small-estate procedures let many estates avoid full probate. Most surprise probate proceedings come from one of three small structural failures — an unfunded asset, a stale beneficiary designation, or a joint owner who predeceased — each of which is preventable in an afternoon of careful titling.

PART II

THE OPENING MONTHS

The first thirty days, the personal representative, and the calendar that begins to set itself.

CHAPTER 3

The First 30 Days After Death

Chapter at a Glance

- Why the first month after death feels like a wall — and why the wall is the system functioning.
- What can be done in week one, week two, and weeks three through five.
- Why banks freeze accounts the moment a death is reported, and what document changes that.
- Six specific things to do during the wait that pay back many times over.
- Five specific things not to do during the wait, even when the family agrees.

The first month after a death is usually the most confusing month of an estate. Families often arrive at this period with the wrong expectation. They expect that someone — a lawyer, a court, an executor — will quickly take charge, that a process will begin to visibly move, that the affairs of the deceased will start to feel orderly within a few weeks. None of that is what happens.

What happens, in nearly every case, is that the family waits.

This is the period in which probate begins. It does not begin with a courtroom appearance. It begins with the slow, document-by-document assembly of the things the court will eventually need: a death certificate in multiple original copies, the original will (if one exists), an account of the deceased's known assets, a preliminary list of debts, and the identity of the person who is about to step into the role of executor or administrator. None of this is glamorous. Almost none of it can be rushed.

Understanding this rhythm in advance prevents most of the frustration that first-time executors and grieving family members otherwise feel.

Day One Through Day Seven

The first week's work is typically practical, not legal. It includes:

- obtaining the death certificate from the funeral home or the vital-records office (multiple originals, usually ten to fifteen),
- locating the original will and any related estate-planning documents (trust agreement, durable power of attorney, advance directives, letter of instruction),
- notifying the immediate family and close associates,
- securing the deceased's residence (locks, mail, perishable items, pets, vehicles),

- identifying the deceased's primary financial relationships (bank, brokerage, payroll, retirement custodian, insurance carriers),
- preserving access to digital accounts where the deceased's plan permits.

Note what is not on this list. There is no court filing in week one. There is no probate hearing in week one. There is, in nearly every case, no formal legal authority yet vested in any family member. Everything in week one is done either by the deceased's pre-existing standing arrangements (a joint owner who can still operate a joint account, a named beneficiary who can begin a claim) or by the family acting informally on behalf of the deceased's interests, in good faith, before any court has spoken.

Day Eight Through Day Thirty

By the second and third weeks, the work begins to take a more procedural shape. The family or the named executor consults a probate attorney (or, in smaller estates, the probate court's self-help office). A petition for probate is drafted. The original will is lodged with the court. Notice is given to the persons entitled to notice — typically the heirs and beneficiaries. A hearing is scheduled, usually four to eight weeks out, at which the court will admit the will to probate and formally appoint the personal representative.

During this same period, banks and brokerages are notified of the death. Most institutions freeze the deceased's individual accounts immediately upon notification. Joint accounts may continue to operate. Beneficiary-designated accounts begin their own internal claims process, separate from probate. Direct deposits stop. Automatic payments may continue, sometimes inappropriately, until someone with authority cancels them. The estate during this window is in a kind of suspended animation: present but inaccessible, owned but unmoving.

Why Banks Won't Help Yet

The single most common source of frustration in the first thirty days is the bank's refusal to release any of the deceased's funds. Family members find this incomprehensible — there are bills to pay, a funeral to settle, a mortgage that just came due. They have the death certificate. They have a copy of the will. The bank will not act.

The bank is not being difficult. The bank is being prudent.

Until a court formally appoints a personal representative, there is no person with legal authority to act for the deceased's individual accounts. If the bank releases funds to someone who turns out not to be the appointed executor, the bank is liable. That liability is real, it has been litigated for centuries, and bank operations procedures reflect it. Banks know that they will not be sued for waiting. They will be sued for releasing too early.

What the bank will accept, almost universally, is one document: the Letters Testamentary or Letters of Administration issued by the probate court. With those Letters in hand, the personal representative can present themselves at the branch and conduct ordinary business — open an estate account, transfer funds, close accounts, redirect mail. Without those Letters, the bank has no defensible basis on which to release a single dollar.

> **KEY POINT**
>
> The thirty days between death and the formal appointment of the personal representative are designed by the system to keep someone from acting too quickly. The wait is the system, not a malfunction of it.

What Can Be Done During the Wait

Even though formal authority has not been issued, several practical and useful things can be done in the first month:

1. **Order original death certificates.** Order ten to fifteen originals. Every financial institution will want an original or a certified copy; photocopies are not accepted.
2. **Lodge the will.** Most states require the original will to be filed (lodged) with the probate court within a short window after death. This is administrative filing only — it does not begin the probate proceeding itself.
3. **Open an estate file.** Begin a single binder or digital folder containing the death certificate, the will, the trust

agreement, account statements, insurance policies, the deed and title documents, the most recent tax return, and any letter of instruction. The personal representative and the attorney will need all of these in the next phase.

4. **Identify and freeze risk.** Cancel credit cards, freeze credit reports against fraud, redirect mail to the executor's address, secure the residence, and instruct the post office to hold delivery. Identity theft against the deceased is a real and growing problem in the first ninety days after death.

5. **Pay only what must be paid.** Mortgage payments, utility payments on the residence, and reasonable funeral expenses can be made from non-estate sources (a surviving spouse's account, a beneficiary disbursement, the executor's own funds with later reimbursement). Ordinary credit-card debt should wait — it becomes a creditor claim in due course.

6. **Consult counsel.** Most probate counsel will meet with the family in the first two weeks at low or no cost to evaluate the estate and recommend a path. That conversation often saves significant money in subsequent filings.

What Should Not Be Done During the Wait

Several things commonly attempted in the first month produce more trouble than they prevent. They are:

- Distributing personal property among family members "the way she would have wanted." Until inventory is taken and the estate is administered, premature distribution can constitute conversion. It can also produce disputes that did not exist before the distribution started.
- Closing accounts unilaterally. The personal representative, once appointed, will need to close them in a documented sequence. Closing them before appointment scrambles the audit trail.
- Selling property, even when the family agrees. The right to sell estate property arises with the appointment of the personal representative and, in some states, only after specific court authorization.
- Talking to creditors at length. Creditors should be referred to the executor or the executor's counsel once appointment occurs. The family member who tries to negotiate with a credit-card company at week two often makes representations that complicate the later claim process.
- Posting the death broadly on social media before the family has decided how to handle it. Identity-theft rings monitor obituary feeds. They begin opening fraudulent accounts within days.

The Emotional Mismatch

The first thirty days create a peculiar disorientation that is rarely named directly. The family is in mourning. The deceased's name and presence are everywhere. There is a need to do something, anything, to feel that the person's affairs are being honored. And the legal system answers that need with a thirty-day pause that requires the family to mostly not act.

What This Looks Like in Practice

The day after his father died, a man we will call David tries to pay the cable bill for the family home using his father's checking account. The auto-pay had failed because the bank had received notice of the death from the cable company's automated system the morning of the death. The account was now frozen.

David is not yet the executor. The will is on its way to the lawyer; the petition for probate has not been drafted; Letters Testamentary will not issue for at least five weeks. The bank tells David, politely, that they cannot release any funds. They explain that the account has not been seized — it is simply frozen until the appointed personal representative can present Letters.

David is initially angry. By the end of week two, after a conversation with the lawyer, he understands that the bank's freeze is doing exactly what it should be doing. If the bank had released funds to David — or to anyone — and the will turned out to name a different executor, the bank would be exposed. The freeze is the bank's protection and, indirectly, the family's. It also, in this case, prevents David's older brother — who has produced a ten-year-old document claiming to be a more recent will — from accessing the account in the meantime.

David pays the cable bill from his own funds and notes the amount for later reimbursement. The estate, when finally administered, reimburses him in full. The freeze, which felt punitive in the first week, turns out to have prevented exactly the kind of early-stage fraud the system is designed to prevent.

This mismatch is one of the principal reasons probate has its difficult reputation. The system is operating exactly as intended. The family experiences it as a wall. Both views are correct.

Notes on Practice

A particular question arises so often in the first thirty days that it deserves its own treatment: what about the deceased's pets.

Pets are personal property under American law. They are not, for legal purposes, beneficiaries. A pet cannot inherit. A pet's care, however, is often the most immediately pressing non-financial concern in the days after a death. The deceased's letter of instruction may name a caregiver. The will may include a pet-trust provision (in states that recognize pet trusts). In most cases, however, no formal arrangement exists, and the family must improvise.

The right immediate move is the practical one: identify a caregiver willing to take the pet, transfer custody promptly, and document the transfer with a brief written note that the executor will eventually file with the inventory. The pet's ongoing food, veterinary, and boarding expenses are estate expenses if the executor agrees to pay them; many executors do, particularly when the eventual beneficiary is a family member who will continue caring for the animal.

What is unhelpful is to treat the pet as a freestanding controversy. The pet's needs are immediate; the question of who eventually pays for the pet's care can be resolved later, calmly, in the regular accounting.

The most useful thing a family member can do in the first thirty days is to understand that the wait is, in fact, the work. Documents are being gathered. Notice is being prepared. The court calendar is moving on its own schedule. By the time the first probate hearing is held — typically four to eight weeks after death — most of the foundation work for the entire administration has already been done. The hearing itself, in an uncontested case, often lasts five minutes. The five minutes is the visible tip of a month of preparation.

> **KEY POINT**
>
> The first thirty days of an estate are an active waiting period. Documents are gathered. Notice is prepared. The court calendar is moving. The visible inactivity is the preparation that will make the eventual hearing routine.

What This Chapter Has Said

The first thirty days create a peculiar tension between a family's need to act and the system's requirement to wait. The wait is purposeful. Letters Testamentary do not issue until the court has admitted the will and confirmed the executor's appointment, which typically does not happen until week six through ten. Banks and brokerages cannot release funds before Letters issue. Useful work in the meantime focuses on documents, security, and engagement of counsel. Premature distribution, sales, and creditor negotiations are best deferred until authority has been formally vested.

CHAPTER 4

The Role of the Executor or Personal Representative

Chapter at a Glance

- The terminology — executor, administrator, personal representative — explained without legalese.
- The full eight-step duty cycle of an executor, from petition to discharge.
- What an executor cannot do, no matter what the family asks.
- Compensation regimes by state, and why family-member executors often waive the fee.
- When and how to decline the role gracefully, and why declining is sometimes the most responsible choice.

The executor is one of the most consequential roles in private American law, and it is also one of the least understood. The person who agrees to serve as executor — usually a spouse, an adult child, a sibling, or a close friend named in the will — almost always agrees without a clear sense of what the role actually requires.

It is worth saying directly, at the outset, what the executor is and is not.

The executor is not a beneficiary advocate.

The executor is not a family referee.

The executor is not the deceased's representative in negotiation with the heirs.

The executor is a court-recognized administrator with a fiduciary duty running primarily to the estate itself and to the people legally entitled to receive from it. That duty is enforceable. It is enforceable in court, by a beneficiary or creditor, against the executor personally. Executors who treat the role casually find this out at exactly the moment they wished they had not.

Two Names for the Same Role

The terminology varies by state, and it confuses readers more than it should. The basic idea is the same. The role is the same. The labels move around.

Table 4.1

Term	When applied	Source
Executor	When named in a valid will and confirmed by the court	Traditional common-law term; still used in most states.
Executrix	Female-form variant; largely retired in modern practice	Older terminology, retained in some state codes.
Personal Representative	Modern unified term covering both will and intestate cases	Uniform Probate Code; many state codes.
Administrator	When there is no will and the court appoints a representative	Common-law term.
Administrator with Will Annexed (administrator c.t.a.)	When there is a will but the named executor cannot serve	Traditional Latin term still used.
Special Administrator	Temporary or limited-purpose appointee	Used during contested cases or for a single asset.

Common terms for the person who administers an estate.

We will use "executor" throughout when referring to a will-named appointee and "personal representative" as the inclusive term covering both will and intestate cases. The duties are the same.

What the Executor Actually Does

The job is wide and detailed. In rough chronology, an executor's duties look like this:

1. **Petition the court.** File the petition for probate, present the original will, and request appointment as personal representative. Notice is provided to the heirs and

beneficiaries. A hearing is held — in uncontested cases, a brief one. The court issues Letters Testamentary.

2. **Take inventory.** Identify and value all probate assets as of the date of death. This becomes the formal Inventory and Appraisal filed with the court — the document that defines the universe the estate is administering.

3. **Provide notice to creditors.** Publish notice in a newspaper of record (in most states) and provide direct notice to known creditors. This opens the creditor-claim window.

4. **Manage estate assets.** Open an estate bank account. Collect rent, interest, dividends. Pay ongoing expenses (mortgage, utilities, insurance, property tax). Preserve property. Liquidate where authorized. The executor stands in the financial shoes of the deceased for the duration of the administration.

5. **Evaluate and pay claims.** Review creditor claims as they arrive. Pay valid ones. Reject invalid ones. Negotiate doubtful ones, with court approval where required.

6. **File tax returns.** File the deceased's final personal income-tax return for the year of death. File the estate's annual income-tax returns (Form 1041). File the federal estate-tax return (Form 706) if required. File any state estate or inheritance tax returns required.

7. **Distribute.** After debts, taxes, and expenses are paid, prepare a final accounting for the court. Petition for distribution. Distribute the remaining property to the beneficiaries as directed by the will (or by intestate law).

8. **Close.** Petition the court for discharge. The court approves the final accounting and the executor is released from further duty. The estate is closed.

Each of these steps has its own paperwork, its own deadlines, and its own procedural rules. None is exotic. None requires extraordinary expertise. Most experienced probate counsel can guide a first-time executor through all eight steps in a routine case in three to four extended meetings spread across nine to twelve months.

What the Executor Cannot Do

It is at least as important to understand the limits of the role. The executor cannot:

- Reinterpret the will. The will means what its words mean, applied by the court if there is ambiguity. The executor's preferences are not relevant.
- Reinterpret intestate succession. If there is no will, the state's intestate-succession statute controls who takes. The executor cannot deviate from it.
- Pay one beneficiary before another. Distributions follow the priority order established by statute and the will, after

debts and claims. Skipping the queue creates personal liability.

- Sell property at a discount to a family member without court authorization. Sales must be at fair value, supported by appraisal where required, and (in many states) noticed to the beneficiaries.
- Compromise with a creditor outside the claim process. The claim process exists for a reason; settlements outside it are unenforceable against the estate.
- Hold the assets indefinitely. The court expects administration to progress on a reasonable timeline. An executor who sits on assets without action invites a beneficiary's petition to compel.
- Refuse to account. Beneficiaries are entitled, by statute, to a formal accounting before final distribution. The executor's view that the family already "knows what's going on" is not a substitute.

KEY POINT

The executor is accountable to the court, to the law, and to the estate itself. The executor is not free to "just do what seems fair." Where intuitive fairness conflicts with legal duty, legal duty controls.

Compensation

Executors are entitled to compensation in nearly every state. The specific amount depends on whether the will provides a number, on local statutes, and on the complexity of the administration.

Table 4.2

State	Default mechanism	Typical range
California	Statutory percentage on appraised gross estate	≈ 4% on first $100k, declining tiers thereafter.
New York	Statutory percentage commission	≈ 5% on first $100k, declining tiers.
Florida	"Reasonable compensation" by statute	Defaults to 3% of inventory value.
Texas	"Reasonable compensation," no statutory percentage	Often 5% in/out of estate; court can adjust.
Illinois	Reasonable compensation	Court-supervised determination.
Pennsylvania	"Reasonable compensation," case-law schedules	Tiered schedule, ≈ 5% on first $100k.

Selected executor-compensation regimes (figures change; verify with current state law).

Family executors often waive compensation, especially when they are also the principal beneficiary. Waiving makes economic sense in those cases — fees paid to the executor are taxable as ordinary income, while distributions to the same person as a beneficiary are not. We will return to this in Chapter 7.

Personal Liability

Executors who follow the procedure are protected. Executors who depart from it are exposed.

An executor who pays the wrong creditor, distributes to the wrong beneficiary, sells property below value, fails to file a required tax return, or commingles estate assets with their own is personally liable for the loss. The fiduciary surety bond — required in many states unless waived in the will — covers some categories of loss but not others. Insurance is available but expensive. The cleanest path is also the simplest: follow the procedure, document every step, and consult counsel on anything that feels uncertain.

When Family Tension Arises

Family tension during a probate administration almost always arises from one of three places, and it is worth naming them directly:

1. **Misaligned expectations.** A beneficiary expected a particular item, or a particular amount, and the will or the inventory does not deliver it. The executor is not the cause; the executor is the messenger.
2. **Slow communication.** A beneficiary feels they are being kept in the dark. The administration is moving on the legal calendar, but the family expected updates on the calendar of grief, which is faster. A monthly status note

from the executor — even a short one — eliminates most of this category.

3. **Real conflict.** Disputed assets, contested wills, blended-family disputes, accusations of pre-death undue influence. These are not solved by the executor personally. They are solved by the procedure, with the executor remaining strictly neutral and letting the court decide. We treat this in Chapter 7.

Executors who treat themselves as advocates for one branch of the family invariably make the dispute worse. Executors who treat themselves as procedural neutrals — even at the cost of being told they are being "cold" — almost always close the estate cleanly.

Should You Accept the Role

If you have been named in a will and you are not sure whether to accept, the questions to ask are practical:

- Do you have nine to eighteen months of bandwidth to handle administrative work, intermittently, for the duration?
- Are you prepared to be the visible decision-maker for distributions that some family members may dislike?
- Are you able to consult counsel and follow counsel's advice even when family pressure runs the other way?
- Are you willing to keep careful records, file required documents on time, and account formally to the beneficiaries

at the close?

What This Looks Like in Practice

Margaret, an executor for her late husband's estate, faces a decision in month four. The estate is in good shape. Letters issued in week six. The inventory has been filed. The creditor window is still open. Two of the children — both adult, both named in the will as residuary beneficiaries — have begun to ask her for early distributions. They have personal expenses they would like to address. They believe the estate is solvent. They want, in essence, an advance.

Margaret's instinct is to help. She is, after all, their mother. The estate's lawyer, in a single conversation, explains why she should not.

First, the creditor-claim window is still open. A creditor she has not yet identified could surface in the next two months and present a valid claim. If she has already distributed the asset the creditor would have reached, she may be personally liable to make the creditor whole. Second, partial distributions complicate the eventual final accounting and can produce the appearance of preferential treatment among siblings. Third, even if the partial distribution is uncontested today, family circumstances may change before the closing — and the partial distribution becomes a leverage point in any subsequent disagreement.

Margaret, after the conversation, declines the children's request and explains why. She offers, instead, a written commitment to make a meaningful distribution as soon as the creditor window has closed and the tax position is clear. The children understand. The estate eventually closes in month eleven with a clean accounting and no intra-family complaint. Margaret has done the executor's job — even at the cost of a difficult conversation in month four.

If the answer is no on any of these, decline. Declining is permitted. The will typically names a successor executor; if not, the court appoints one based on statutory priority. Declining a role you cannot perform well is an act of integrity, not a failure.

Notes on Practice

Three subtler dimensions of the executor's role appear less often in published treatments and deserve a brief note.

The first is the executor's relationship with the estate's lawyer. The lawyer represents the executor in the executor's fiduciary capacity. The lawyer does not represent the executor personally. If the executor's individual interests diverge from the estate's — for example, in a question of executor compensation or a disputed reimbursement — the executor may need separate counsel. Most experienced probate counsel raise this distinction proactively at the first meeting.

The second is the executor's posture when family members press for early information. Pre-appointment, the executor has no formal authority. Post-appointment, the executor has duties of disclosure to beneficiaries but not yet to other family members. Adult nieces, in-laws, longtime friends — all may ask questions in good faith, but their entitlement to information is not automatic. The executor's safest posture is to communicate generously with named beneficiaries and minimally with everyone else, not because privacy is the goal but because the duty runs only where the law says it runs.

The third is the executor's emotional exposure during the administration. Executors typically hold a complicated combination of grief and responsibility for nine to eighteen months. Many executors find this draining in ways they did not expect. The work is best paced. Important decisions are best made unhurried. If the executor needs to take time off from the role for personal reasons, most courts will allow a co-executor or special administrator to be appointed for the interval. The role is not designed to be carried alone in every moment.

If the answer is yes, take it. The role is unglamorous, painstaking, and often genuinely meaningful. A family that is well-served by its executor remembers it for a generation. A family that is poorly served by its executor remembers that for two.

Figure 4.1

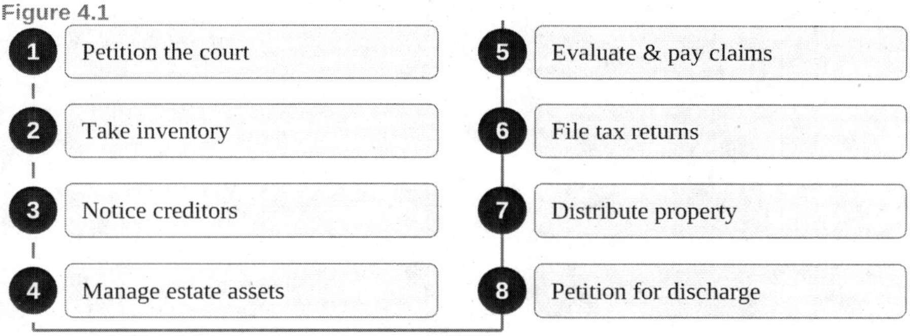

The executor's eight-step duty cycle, from petition to discharge.

> **KEY POINT**
>
> The executor is not a beneficiary advocate or a family referee. The executor is a court-recognized fiduciary whose duties run to the estate and the law. Treating the role with that clarity protects the executor, the estate, and — over the longer arc — the family relationships.

What This Chapter Has Said

The executor's role is wide and structured: from petition for probate through inventory, creditor notice, claim evaluation, tax filings, distribution, and discharge. The role carries real fiduciary duty enforceable in court. Compensation is available; many family executors waive it. Personal liability attaches to executors who depart from procedure. The cleanest path is also the simplest: follow the procedure, document every step, and consult counsel on anything that feels uncertain. Family tension during administration is normal and is largely manageable through clear, consistent communication.

PART III

◆

THE COURT AND THE CALENDAR

What the court actually does, and why probate moves at the pace it does.

CHAPTER 5

What the Court Actually Does (and Doesn't Do)

Chapter at a Glance

- The five things the probate court actually does — and the much longer list of things it does not.
- Why probate looks slow from outside even when nothing is going wrong inside.
- The institutional limits of the court's compassion, and why that limit is a feature.
- Two common misconceptions about court power that produce avoidable disappointment.
- When a case naturally produces more court involvement, and how to know in advance whether yours will.

The probate court is the most visible institution in the entire process, and it is also the most widely misunderstood one. Families arrive at the courthouse, in person or through their counsel, expecting that the judge will manage the estate, evaluate the family's needs, weigh in on whether the executor is doing a good job, and ultimately decide who gets what. None of those things is the court's job.

The probate court does not manage estates. It supervises them. The distinction matters more than it sounds.

The Five Things the Court Actually Does

If we strip the procedure to its essentials, the probate court does five things, in this order, across the life of an estate:

1. **Confirms authority.** The court reviews the will, finds it valid, and issues Letters Testamentary appointing the executor. Or, in the absence of a will, the court reviews the petition of the person seeking to administer the estate, applies the statutory priority order, and issues Letters of Administration. This is the court's first act, and it is what creates the personal representative as a recognized legal actor.

2. **Polices the procedure.** The court ensures that required notices have gone out, that the creditor-claim window has been opened correctly, that the inventory has been filed within the statutory deadline, and that the estate's filings (interim accountings, status reports, tax-related notices) are made on time and in the required form. This work is largely clerical from the court's side; it becomes adjudicative only when something is missing or contested.

3. **Resolves disputes.** When a will is contested, when a creditor's claim is rejected and the creditor sues, when beneficiaries disagree about a distribution, when there is a

question of whether the executor breached fiduciary duty — the court adjudicates. This is the part of probate that looks like television. It is also the part that almost never happens. The great majority of estates close without a single contested matter ever reaching the bench.

4. **Approves significant transactions.** Sales of real estate, sales of business interests, settlements of litigation, payment of disputed claims, and (in many states) advance distributions to beneficiaries before the close all require court approval, often after notice to the interested parties. The court's role here is procedural — making sure the proposed action is regular and noticed — rather than substantive.

5. **Approves the closing.** When the executor has done their work, the executor petitions the court for approval of the final accounting and authorization of the final distribution. The court reviews the accounting, hears any objections, and either approves or directs corrections. After approval, the estate is closed and the executor is discharged.

Everything else that happens in a probate administration happens between those five court touch points. Inventory is taken between Steps 1 and 2. Creditors are paid between Steps 2 and 4. Tax returns are filed in the background. Investments are managed. Real estate is preserved or sold. Correspondence flows between the executor's office and the beneficiaries. The court is, for most of this work, not involved.

What the Court Does Not Do

It is at least as important to understand the long list of things the court is not in the business of doing. The court does not:

- Investigate the deceased's estate on its own initiative. The court does not look for hidden assets. It evaluates what the executor reports.
- Value personal property. Furniture, jewelry, art, collectibles — the executor (with appraiser support where useful) values these. The court accepts the inventory unless someone objects.
- Mediate family disagreements. Family meetings, sibling negotiations, blended-family conversations — the court is not present in any of these unless a formal proceeding is filed.
- Audit creditor claims for substantive accuracy. The executor evaluates whether a claim is owed; the court intervenes only on a rejection-and-suit basis.
- Provide tax advice. The court does not interpret the Internal Revenue Code. The estate's tax compliance is the executor's responsibility, with counsel.
- Track the deceased's intent beyond the four corners of the will. The will's words mean what they say; extrinsic evidence is admitted only when the words are ambiguous,

and even then under tightly drawn rules.

- Continue to oversee anything after the closing. Once the estate is closed, the court's involvement ends. Subsequent disputes among beneficiaries are matters for civil litigation, not probate.

Why Probate Looks Slow

From the outside, probate looks slow because the court appears between long intervals of nothing. The hearing in week six is followed by no court activity at all until the inventory is filed in month four. Then the next milestone is the closing of the creditor-claim window, typically in month seven or eight. Then the petition for distribution, typically in month ten or eleven. Each gap is silent from the court's perspective. From the executor's perspective, those gaps are full of work — inventory, valuation, creditor evaluation, tax preparation. From the family's perspective, those gaps look like inactivity.

This is one of the principal sources of frustration that produces the perception of probate as a lethargic system. The court is not lethargic. The court is, in fact, scheduled. The work between the court's appearances is the work that makes the court's eventual approval routine. An executor who does the in-between work well closes the estate faster than one who does not.

The Limits of the Court's Sympathy

Families occasionally arrive at the probate court expecting a compassionate audience. The deceased was a parent; the family is grieving; the relationships are strained; the situation is, in real human terms, hard. They expect the judge to acknowledge this and to calibrate the procedure accordingly.

The judge does not. The court does not.

This is not callousness. It is the court's institutional posture. Probate is one of the few areas of American law where the court is asked to administer something — to operate a procedure, to confirm a set of orderly steps — rather than to decide between adversaries. The court's discipline lies in not weighing the human factors that the family is so aware of. The court is operating on the assumption that the law's procedural fairness is what the family will eventually be grateful for, even if it is not the source of comfort in the moment.

> **REFLECTION**
>
> The probate court is built to be the same court whether the family is in harmony or in fracture. That sameness is not a limitation. It is the institution's most reliable feature.

Two Common Misconceptions

Two beliefs about the probate court appear so frequently that they are worth correcting directly.

The first is that the probate court can "speed things up" for a family that is in particular need. It cannot. The court's calendar is structured around statutory waiting periods (the creditor-claim window, the notice period for petitions, the time-to-respond on objections). Those periods are statutory; they are not within the judge's discretion. An estate cannot be closed before the creditor-claim window has expired, no matter how united the family is or how clean the administration is.

The second is that the probate court will protect a beneficiary against an unfair distribution. The court enforces the will's terms. If the will distributes ninety percent to one child and ten percent to another, the court will enforce that. The court does not have authority to redistribute on the basis of perceived fairness. A beneficiary who believes the will reflects undue influence, fraud, or lack of capacity may file a will contest — but that is a separate, contested proceeding with significant evidentiary burdens, and it is rarely won.

When Court Involvement Increases

Three categories of estate produce more court involvement than ordinary cases:

1. **Contested estates.** Will contests, removal petitions against the executor, claim rejections that go to litigation. These cases involve repeated appearances, evidentiary hearings, sometimes trial.

2. **Court-supervised states.** A handful of states still default to formal supervision of all probate cases — every transaction approved in advance. Most states have moved toward independent or unsupervised administration, which keeps the court out of routine matters. Knowing which kind of supervision applies in your jurisdiction is the single most important predictor of timeline and cost.
3. **Estates with minor or incapacitated beneficiaries.** When a beneficiary is a minor, has a disability, or is otherwise under a guardianship, the court remains involved beyond the closing to oversee the beneficiary's share until the disability ends or a trust is funded. This is a separate proceeding running in parallel.

What All This Means in Practice

What This Looks Like in Practice

A first-time executor, eight months into administering his late mother's estate, asks the probate-court clerk a question. The estate has a piece of artwork his sister wants to keep. The art has not been formally appraised. His sister has offered the estate three thousand dollars for it; he believes it is worth closer to fifteen thousand. He wants the court to decide.

The clerk listens politely and says, with no irritation, that this is not what the court does.

If the executor and the beneficiary cannot agree on the appraised value, the executor's options are clear: hire a qualified appraiser, document the appraisal, propose a distribution that reflects the appraised value, and petition the court for approval if the beneficiary objects. Only at the petition stage does the court engage. And even then, the court is not asked to value the artwork on its own; it is asked to review whether the executor's procedure was regular.

The executor leaves the courthouse with a clear sense of what he needs to do next. He hires an appraiser. The appraiser values the artwork at fourteen thousand dollars. The sister, presented with the appraisal, accepts it and pays the estate the appraised amount. The executor never returns to the courthouse on this question. The court — by not involving itself — has done its job.

The practical takeaway from this chapter is simple. The court is not a participant in the day-to-day life of an estate. It is a series of scheduled checkpoints. Between the checkpoints, the executor is the estate, and the estate moves at whatever pace the executor (with counsel) is able to maintain. A capable executor working with capable counsel can move an uncontested estate through all five court touch points in eight to twelve months. A disorganized executor can stretch the same estate to two or three years.

Notes on Practice

Probate courts vary considerably in their day-to-day operation, and a few practical observations are worth recording.

Some probate courts handle hundreds of matters a week and operate almost entirely on filed paper, with hearings reserved for contested issues. Others retain a more hands-on tradition: every petition reviewed in chambers, every accounting examined on the bench, every settlement requiring the judge's signed comfort. The first kind — common in large urban counties — tends to produce faster but more impersonal cases. The second kind — common in smaller jurisdictions — tends to produce slower but more carefully reviewed cases.

Neither model is intrinsically better than the other. They produce different experiences. Counsel familiar with the particular court's rhythm can usually predict, within a few weeks, how long a particular case will take. Counsel unfamiliar with the local rhythm — for example, a generalist lawyer handling a single probate matter for a long-time client — often misjudges the calendar by months. Engaging local probate counsel, even on a limited-scope basis, is one of the highest-yield decisions a family can make.

The court is not the bottleneck in either case.

KEY POINT

The probate court is not a participant in the day-to-day life of an estate. It is a series of scheduled checkpoints. Between the checkpoints, the executor is the estate. The pace is set by the work the executor does in the long quiet weeks between hearings.

What This Chapter Has Said

The probate court does five things across the life of an estate: confirms authority, polices the procedure, resolves disputes, approves significant transactions, and approves the closing. It does not investigate, mediate, value personal property, audit creditor claims for substance, give tax advice, or read intent into ambiguous wills beyond the rules that allow it. Its calendar is structured by statute. Its compassion is delivered through the steady, predictable operation of procedure rather than through individual engagement. That posture — uniform, reliable, indifferent — is the institution's most valuable feature.

CHAPTER 6

Why Probate Takes So Long

Chapter at a Glance

- The four largely fixed inputs that set the floor of any probate timeline.
- The variable input — estate complexity — and how to estimate it before opening the case.
- Seven recurring sources of avoidable delay that account for most cases that overrun.
- Five operational habits that consistently produce faster closings.
- Realistic timelines by estate type, including small estates, contested estates, and estates with business interests.

The single most common question families ask probate counsel is some version of: how long will this take. The honest answer is almost always longer than the family expects, and it is rarely because anything has gone wrong.

Probate duration is a function of four largely fixed inputs and one highly variable input. The fixed inputs cannot be shortened. The variable input is where most of the actual control lies.

The Four Fixed Inputs

The fixed inputs are statutory. They are the same in a one-million-dollar estate and a ten-million-dollar estate, and they are the same whether the family is harmonious or in conflict. They are:

1. **The notice period for opening the estate.** Most states require that notice of the petition for probate be given to interested parties — heirs, beneficiaries, sometimes creditors — at least a specified number of days before the hearing. Common windows are fifteen, twenty, or thirty days. The hearing cannot be advanced. This typically locks the first hearing into the fourth-to-eighth week after death.

2. **The creditor-claim window.** After the executor publishes notice to creditors, statute prescribes a period during which creditors must present claims. This is the largest single timing input in probate. The window varies by state but is most commonly four to six months from publication.

3. **Tax-return windows.** The deceased's final personal-income-tax return is due on the ordinary calendar (April 15 of the year after death, with extension available). The federal estate-tax return, when required, is due nine months after death (with a six-month extension available). Some state estate or inheritance tax returns have shorter or longer windows. None of these can be accelerated.

4. **The court's calendar between filings.** Probate calendars are not light. From petition for distribution to actual hearing date is typically four to six weeks in busy courts; longer in some metropolitan jurisdictions.

If you sum the minimums in a typical case, you arrive at the floor of an uncontested probate: roughly six to nine months from death to closing, even when nothing is in dispute and everyone is cooperating fully. The fixed inputs alone account for that floor.

Table 6.1

State	Claim window	Notice trigger
California	4 months	From issuance of Letters.
Florida	3 months from publication / 30 days from served notice	Either method controls.
Texas	4 months	From publication of notice to creditors.
New York	7 months	From issuance of Letters.
Illinois	6 months	From publication.
Pennsylvania	1 year	From decedent's death (with public notice).
Nevada	60 days from notice / 90 days from publication	Whichever is later.
Ohio	6 months	From decedent's death.

Selected creditor-claim windows by state (verify with current law).

The Variable Input — Estate Complexity

Above the fixed floor sits the variable input: the time required to do the actual administrative work. This depends on:

- the number and type of assets in the inventory,
- whether real property exists and whether it must be sold,
- whether business interests exist and whether they require valuation,
- the number of jurisdictions involved (an out-of-state property triggers an ancillary proceeding),
- the volume and complexity of creditor claims,
- tax complexity (federal estate tax, state estate or inheritance tax, business interests requiring valuation discounts, retirement accounts requiring careful sequencing of distributions),
- whether the will is contested or any beneficiary objects to any step,
- the diligence of the executor and the responsiveness of the executor's counsel.

An estate consisting of a house, a brokerage account, two bank accounts, and a car typically clears the variable work in three or four months on top of the fixed floor — a total of eight to ten months. An estate with a closely held business, real property in three states, an estate-tax return, and a contested codicil can take three years.

Common Sources of Avoidable Delay

Independent of the fixed inputs and the inherent complexity, several specific factors regularly add months to probate cases unnecessarily. They are worth naming because most can be avoided:

1. **Missing original will.** If the original cannot be found, the estate may be administered as intestate, or the proponent may attempt to admit a copy with a presumption-of-revocation rebuttal. Both paths add weeks of motion practice.

2. **Incomplete inventory.** Forgotten accounts, late-discovered safe-deposit boxes, subsequently-found life-insurance policies — each requires the inventory to be amended and notice to be re-given on the amendment. Each amendment can add four to six weeks.

3. **Slow creditor evaluation.** Some claims are obvious; others require investigation. Executors who take three months to evaluate a claim that should have taken two weeks delay the entire administration.

4. **Real-estate sale negotiation.** Selling estate property at fair value takes the time it takes. Forced sales often produce litigation. Patient sales sometimes extend the administration by months — but the alternative is worse.

5. **Tax filings out of order.** Filing the federal estate-tax return late (when one is required) produces penalty

exposure and freezes the petition for distribution until the IRS issues a closing letter or the administrator can certify timely filing.

6. **Beneficiary disagreements over personal property.** Tangible personal property — furniture, jewelry, photographs, memorabilia — is statistically the most common source of intra-family dispute, and the most preventable. We treat this in Chapter 7.

7. **Out-of-state real property.** Triggers a separate ancillary probate in the other state. The ancillary case has its own timeline, its own creditor window, and its own court.

What Speeds Probate Up

There is no magic, but there are habits. The estates that close fastest tend to share five operational characteristics:

1. **Organized records before the death.** An identified file (paper or digital) listing accounts, advisors, attorneys, insurance, real estate, login credentials (in a secure form). Estates with this file close months faster than estates without it.

2. **Counsel engaged in week one or two.** Engaging probate counsel early lets the petition, notice, and creditor publication be prepared cleanly the first time. Estates that try to start without counsel and add counsel in month three almost always pay the cost in calendar weeks.

3. **Professional valuation when needed.** Hiring an appraiser for real estate and business interests early — rather than waiting until pressed by the court — makes the inventory clean and the eventual sale or distribution supportable.
4. **Active executor communication with beneficiaries.** Monthly or bi-monthly written updates to the beneficiaries, even when the update is “the creditor window is still open and we are waiting,” prevent the beneficiary anxiety that produces objections.
5. **Tax planning that anticipates distribution.** An executor who works with a CPA from the early months — rather than retrofitting tax planning at month nine — closes faster, with cleaner allocation of basis, and with fewer post-closing surprises.

Realistic Expectations

What is a realistic expectation, then, for a typical estate?

For an uncontested estate with ordinary assets — a house, a few accounts, a car, household goods — eight to twelve months from death to closing is a normal range. Six to seven months is unusually fast. Eighteen months is not unusual when complexity exists.

For an estate with a closely held business or significant real estate, twelve to twenty-four months is common.

For a contested estate — will contest, removal petition, rejected-claim litigation — three to five years is realistic, and the estate's costs will rise sharply.

Table 6.2

Estate type	Realistic timeline	Principal driver
Small estate (under threshold)	6–10 weeks	Affidavit procedure replaces full probate.
Simple estate, will, no real property	7–9 months	Creditor window + inventory + tax.
Simple estate, will, with real property	9–14 months	Sale or transfer adds months.
Estate with business interests	14–24 months	Valuation and continuity questions.
Estate with multi-state property	12–24 months	Ancillary proceedings in second state.
Estate with federal estate-tax return	15–24 months	Form 706 plus IRS review.
Contested will or major dispute	24–60 months	Litigation calendar dominates.
Intestate estate, simple	10–14 months	Determining heirs adds initial weeks.

Typical probate timelines by estate type.

Why the Long Calendar Is the Point

What This Looks Like in Practice

Two estates open in the same probate court in the same week. Both involve roughly comparable assets — a house, a brokerage account, two retirement accounts, household goods, a car. Neither is contested. Twelve months later, one has closed. The other has not.

The estate that closed had an executor who engaged probate counsel in week one. The petition was filed in week three. Letters issued in week seven. The inventory — completed and verified by an accountant — was filed in month four. Notice to creditors was published the week Letters issued. Tax returns were prepared on schedule. By month eleven, the petition for distribution had been filed and noticed. The court approved the accounting at the month-twelve hearing. The executor distributed and the estate closed.

The estate that did not close had an executor who tried to do the work alone for the first three months. He filed the petition himself in month two; the petition was rejected for an incomplete notice list. He refiled in month three. Letters issued in month four. The inventory was incomplete when first filed and had to be amended twice; each amendment added a notice cycle. The decedent's final tax return was filed late, producing penalties. By month twelve, the executor had engaged counsel and was preparing the petition for distribution. The estate would close, eventually, in month eighteen.

Neither estate was unusual. Neither family was difficult. The difference in calendar — six months — is, in nearly every case like this, the cost of doing the early work alone.

It is tempting to read this chapter and conclude that probate is needlessly slow. It is more accurate to read it and conclude that probate is deliberately slow. The pace exists to surface things — claims, conflicts, mistakes, late-arriving creditors, missed assets — that a faster procedure would conceal. A probate that closes in ten months has had ten months to expose every defect that administration could expose. A probate that closed in three weeks would have done none of that work, and the people relying on it would never know what had been hidden.

Notes on Practice

One operational insight is worth recording in particular: the single estate that closes fastest, statistically, is one in which the deceased prepared a comprehensive letter of instruction during life.

A letter of instruction is not a will. It does not modify the will. It is a non-legal document — typed or handwritten, signed and dated, kept in a known location — that tells the eventual executor where everything is. Where the original will is held. Who the attorney is. Which bank holds the primary account. Which broker holds the investment account. Which insurance carrier holds the life-insurance policy. Which password manager controls the digital accounts. What the deceased's preferences were about funeral arrangements.

Estates that begin with such a letter typically save four to eight weeks of search and reconstruction time at the front of the administration. The savings compound through the rest of the case: a clean inventory comes faster, the creditor evaluation is straightforward, and the tax filings are simpler because the deceased's records are organized.

A sample letter of instruction is provided in Appendix E. It is, plausibly, the highest-leverage single document the estate-planning conversation produces — and it is also the one most often skipped because it is not a billable lawyer task.

Patience, here, is the system functioning.

Figure 6.1

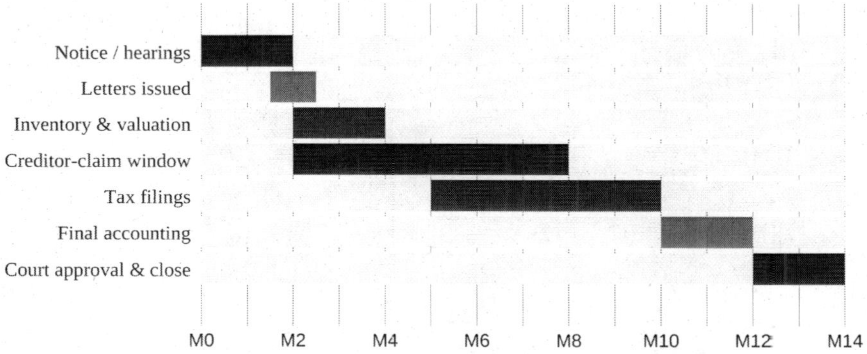

Probate timeline — the four fixed inputs and where they sit on the calendar.

> **KEY POINT**
>
> Eight to twelve months from death to closing is normal for an uncontested estate of ordinary complexity. Faster than that is unusual. Slower than that, in the absence of contest or extraordinary complexity, usually traces to preventable causes.

What This Chapter Has Said

Probate duration is driven by four largely fixed inputs — notice periods, the creditor-claim window, tax-return cycles, the court's own calendar — and one variable input, estate complexity. Above the floor that the fixed inputs set, the variable input dominates. Most cases that overrun do so because of one of seven recurring sources of delay, each of which is largely preventable. Estates that close fastest share five operational habits — early counsel, organized records, professional valuation, active executor communication, and tax planning that anticipates distribution.

PART IV

WHERE THINGS GET STUCK

Delay, dispute, and the misunderstandings that produce both.

CHAPTER 7

What Cases Delays and Disputes

Chapter at a Glance

- The six recurring sources of delay in probate — and why most are about ambiguity, not hostility.
- The three categories of dispute that account for nearly every contested probate.
- The will-contest grounds, their evidentiary burdens, and why most contests fail.
- How no-contest clauses work and how their enforcement varies by state.
- How to prevent the most common distribution disputes with two simple drafting moves.

Most probate cases close on time. Of those that do not, almost all are delayed by one of a small set of recurring problems. The same is true of disputes: most estates have none, and of those that have any, the category of dispute is usually predictable. This chapter names those problems and treats each in turn.

Six Recurring Sources of Delay

After watching enough probate cases unfold, the practitioner notices that delay is not random. Six categories account for nearly every case that takes longer than it should. They are:

1. **Documents are missing.** The original will cannot be found. The trust agreement was executed but the funding documents are not in the file. A safe-deposit-box key cannot be located. A deed was never recorded. Each of these forces the executor to reconstruct what should have been a single afternoon's filing into a multi-week evidentiary effort.

2. **Ownership is unclear.** Title to a property is held by an entity that no longer exists. A joint account has the wrong second name. A business interest is documented in a binder that contradicts the buy-sell agreement. Until ownership is clear, the asset cannot be inventoried, taxed, sold, or distributed.

3. **Beneficiaries disagree.** On valuation, on which child gets which item of personal property, on whether the estate should sell the house or distribute it intact. None of these disagreements is exotic. All of them slow the executor, who must respond to each objection in writing.

4. **Debts are contested.** A creditor presents a claim that the executor believes is invalid. The executor rejects it. The creditor sues. The estate now has a litigation case running in parallel with the administration. The estate cannot close

until the litigation is resolved.

5. **Assets are hard to value.** A closely held business with no public comparables. Real estate in a thin market. A collection (art, wine, vintage cars) without a clear appraisal protocol. Each requires a qualified appraiser and, often, a defended valuation when the IRS or state taxing authority asks for substantiation.
6. **Tax complications surface late.** Returns the deceased never filed. Foreign accounts that were never reported. A business that has been undervalued on prior estate-planning gifts. Each of these can extend an administration by months while the executor cures the prior noncompliance.

Most delays come from ambiguity, not hostility. Clear structure put in place during life — a single binder of documents, retitled accounts, current beneficiary designations, and a brief letter of instruction — reduces the probability of all six categories materially.

Three Recurring Sources of Dispute

When probate cases become contested, the dispute almost always falls into one of three categories:

1. **Will contests.** A beneficiary, or a person who believes they would have been a beneficiary under an earlier or different will, challenges the validity of the offered will. Common grounds: lack of testamentary capacity, undue

influence, fraud, improper execution. Will contests are evidentiary, expensive, and statistically unlikely to succeed. They are also disproportionately damaging to family relationships.

2. **Fiduciary disputes.** A beneficiary alleges that the executor has breached fiduciary duty — by self-dealing, by failure to account, by waste of estate assets, by undue delay. The remedy is a removal petition or a surcharge action. Both are slow. Both are damaging.

3. **Distribution disputes.** Beneficiaries disagree about how the will is to be applied to a particular asset, about valuation for in-kind distribution, about the priority of specific bequests when the estate is short. These disputes look procedural but they are emotional. Personal property — the desk, the wedding band, the photo album — is the most frequent flashpoint.

Will Contests — A Closer Look

Will contests deserve a separate treatment because they are widely feared and rarely successful. The grounds are:

Table 7.1

Ground	Burden	Typical evidence required
Lack of testamentary capacity	On contestant	Medical records at time of execution; witness testimony; treating-physician statement.
Undue influence	On contestant (in most states)	Pattern of isolation; relationship of trust; sudden change in dispositive plan; contemporaneous evidence.
Fraud	On contestant	False representation that induced the will; reliance; clear and convincing evidence.
Improper execution	On contestant	Failure of statutory formalities (witnesses, signature, notarization where required).
Revocation	On contestant (rebuts proponent)	Later will or codicil; evidence of intentional destruction.
Mistake	On contestant	Drafter's error; missing dispositive provision; rare and narrowly construed.

Common will-contest grounds and what each requires.

Most will contests fail. The evidentiary burdens are high, the presumptions favor the will's validity, and courts are reluctant to set aside testamentary intent without strong proof. A contest that succeeds typically rests on contemporaneous medical or witness evidence — not on later family disagreement about who deserves what.

What contests almost always do, however, is impose cost and delay. Even an unsuccessful contest can extend the administration by two years and consume six-figure legal fees from both sides. The secondary effect — the durable damage to family relationships — frequently outlasts the cost.

> **REFLECTION**
>
> The most expensive will contest is the one that produces no change in distribution. The estate is depleted, the calendar is consumed, and the family is left with the same outcome the will originally provided — minus several years and several fortunes.

The No-Contest Clause

Many wills include a no-contest clause (also called an in terrorem clause): a provision that disinherits any beneficiary who challenges the will and loses. The strength of these clauses varies by state.

- Some states (Florida, Indiana) refuse to enforce no-contest clauses entirely.
- Most states enforce them unless the contestant had probable cause to file.
- A few states enforce them strictly, regardless of probable cause.

A well-drafted no-contest clause discourages frivolous challenges. It does not eliminate them. A beneficiary who is willing to lose their share for the chance to litigate is undeterred by the clause.

Fiduciary Disputes — A Closer Look

Beneficiaries who believe an executor is not performing have several remedies short of full removal. They can:

1. **Demand an interim accounting.** Most states allow beneficiaries to request a formal accounting at any time. The executor's response is required and reviewable by the court.

2. **Petition for instructions.** Either party can ask the court to clarify a disputed question. The court's instruction binds the executor.

3. **Petition for removal.** If the executor is in serious breach — self-dealing, misappropriation, complete failure to act — the court can remove and replace. Removal is rare and high-bar.

4. **Sue for surcharge.** After closing, beneficiaries can sue an executor personally for any loss attributable to fiduciary breach. This action survives the closing of the estate.

The cleanest defense for an executor against fiduciary challenges is the same advice given throughout this book: document everything, consult counsel before any close decision, communicate with beneficiaries on a regular schedule, and treat the fiduciary duty as the binding standard it actually is. Executors who behave correctly are almost never successfully challenged. Executors who treat the role casually are.

Distribution Disputes — A Closer Look

These are, statistically, the most common disputes. They are also the most preventable. They typically involve:

- Tangible personal property — items of sentimental value with no clean valuation.
- Real property the family does not agree to sell.
- A business interest the will gives to one beneficiary over another's preferences.
- Investment accounts the executor has held during a price decline (or appreciation), and the question of valuation date.

Two simple drafting moves prevent most distribution disputes:

1. **Specific bequests of named items.** If a particular ring is meant for a particular grandchild, name it. The will should not require interpretation of "my jewelry."
2. **A personal-property memorandum.** Many states recognize a separate, signed memorandum referenced in the will, distributing items of personal property without requiring will republication. The settlor can update it without redrafting the will.

These two devices, used at the time of will preparation, eliminate the most frequent category of probate dispute almost entirely.

What an Executor Cannot Solve

What This Looks Like in Practice

An estate is administered without controversy through month nine. The inventory has been filed. The creditor-claim window has closed. The federal estate-tax return has been filed. The executor — a sibling of the deceased — is preparing the petition for final distribution.

In month ten, a previously absent half-sibling, whom no one in the family had heard from in twenty years, files a will contest. The half-sibling alleges that the will admitted to probate reflects a substantial change made in the deceased's last year of life under the influence of a caretaker. The half-sibling has produced no contemporaneous evidence; their counsel proposes to develop evidence in discovery.

The contest produces an immediate freeze on the petition for distribution. The estate, otherwise ready to close, is held open. The executor must respond. The other beneficiaries are drawn into the litigation. Counsel for both sides take depositions. Medical records are subpoenaed. The estate's administrative costs, modest through month nine, begin to accumulate at litigation pace.

Eighteen months later, the contest is dismissed on summary judgment for failure to produce evidence sufficient to defeat the will's presumption of validity. The half-sibling receives nothing. The executor finally distributes in month thirty-two. The estate has paid more than two hundred thousand dollars in litigation costs. The siblings, who had been close, do not speak for several years afterward.

Most will contests look like this. The substantive outcome is rarely changed. The cost — financial and relational — is borne regardless. This is why a no-contest clause, where enforceable, and a clear letter of explanation accompanying the will, where the disposition is unequal, are among the highest-value drafting moves a settlor can make.

It is worth being honest about what the executor's diligence cannot fix. Probate cannot heal long-standing family fractures. It cannot rebalance the favoritism a parent showed during life. It cannot recover what the deceased did not save. It cannot create love where none was there.

Notes on Practice

Three observations from probate-litigation practice are worth recording for any reader contemplating contesting or defending a contested matter.

First, contests are almost always more expensive than the amount in dispute. A typical contest produces six-figure fees on each side. The estate, which pays the executor's side from estate funds, sees its corpus depleted. The contestant typically pays out of pocket; if they lose, the no-contest clause may apply. Even in a winning contest, the share recovered is often less than the litigation cost. The economics of contesting wills favor the estate's side, and they favor settling.

Second, the most successful contests are those grounded in contemporaneous evidence — medical records from the time of execution, affidavits from witnesses who observed the execution, testimony from disinterested professionals who interacted with the testator. Contests grounded in after-the-fact family inference rarely succeed.

Third, the timing of a contest matters. Most states require contests to be filed within a short window — sometimes as little as ninety days from notice of admission to probate. After the window, the will becomes essentially uncontestable. A potential contestant who is uncertain whether to proceed should consult counsel immediately on receiving notice; waiting until the calendar feels right often forfeits the option entirely.

What probate can do is what it was always built to do: transfer ownership lawfully, account for the work, and close. The executor who keeps to that scope serves the estate well. The executor who tries to expand it almost always finds the work pulling the family further apart, not closer together.

KEY POINT

Most probate disputes are preventable with two simple drafting moves: specific bequests of named items, and a personal-property memorandum that distributes tangible personal property without requiring will republication. Done during life, these eliminate the largest single category of post-death conflict.

What This Chapter Has Said

Six recurring sources of delay (missing documents, unclear ownership, beneficiary disagreement, contested debts, hard-to-value assets, late-surfacing tax complications) and three categories of dispute (will contests, fiduciary disputes, distribution disputes) account for nearly every probate that becomes contentious. Will contests are evidentiary, expensive, and statistically unlikely to succeed. Fiduciary disputes are best prevented by clean executor practice. Distribution disputes — the most common — are prevented at drafting time. What probate cannot do is heal pre-existing fractures; it can only transfer ownership lawfully and let the rest happen elsewhere.

PART V

THE HUMAN SIDE OF PROBATE

Misunderstandings, expectations, and why the process feels personal.

CHAPTER 8

What Families Get Wrong About Probate

Chapter at a Glance

- The ten widely held beliefs about probate that turn out to be incorrect.
- Why each of these beliefs is so durable despite being wrong.
- What each belief actually distorts — the underlying fact the family will eventually meet.
- Three reasons probate misunderstandings outlive their corrections.
- Why correcting these beliefs is the first work of any honest estate-planning conversation.

Most of the friction in probate comes not from the procedure itself, but from a small handful of beliefs that turn out to be incorrect. The beliefs are not ignorant. They are the kind of beliefs that a reasonable adult forms by listening to the surrounding culture. They are picked up from neighbors, from television courtroom dramas, from the marketing of competing financial products, from a single anecdote heard at a dinner party twenty years ago. They sound true. They behave as if true. They produce action, sometimes urgent action, long before they are tested against the actual law.

When these beliefs collide with the procedure, the family experiences the collision as the system failing them. Almost without exception, what is failing is the belief, not the system.

This chapter names the most common of those beliefs and corrects them. It is intentionally short on legal nuance and long on plain explanation. Each item begins with the belief as ordinary readers tend to articulate it.

Misunderstanding 1 — "The Will Avoids Probate"

This is the most widespread error of all, and it produces enormous downstream confusion.

A will does not avoid probate. A will is the document that probate administers. The will is the set of instructions; probate is the court process that gives those instructions force. An estate with a will goes through probate. An estate without a will also goes through probate — except the court applies the state's intestate-succession rules instead of the deceased's preferences.

The instruments that genuinely avoid probate are different. They are:

- a properly funded revocable living trust,
- joint titling with right of survivorship,

- payable-on-death and transfer-on-death beneficiary designations,
- Lady-Bird and other transfer-on-death deeds, where state law allows.

A will plus none of these is a will plus probate. A will plus all of these is, in most cases, a will that never reaches probate at all because there is nothing for it to administer.

Misunderstanding 2 — "The Executor Controls Everything"

The executor controls the procedure. The executor does not control the substance.

The will determines who takes what. The state's probate code determines how disputes are resolved, what notices must be given, what claims are paid, and in what order. The court determines whether the executor's accounting is approved. The executor's authority is real but constrained on every side. The executor cannot rewrite the will, cannot override a beneficiary's statutory rights, and cannot dispense with creditor claims that have been validly presented.

Family members who confront the executor with "you have to give me this because you are the executor" have, in nearly every case, misunderstood the role. The executor's answer — "I am required to follow the will and the law" — is not a brush-off. It is the accurate description of the role.

Misunderstanding 3 — “Probate Means Something Went Wrong”

Probate is a procedure. Procedures do not have moral content. An estate going through probate has not failed any test, and the deceased has not been negligent. Probate happens because property exists in a particular legal form at the moment of death. Most estates have at least some property in that form.

It is true that probate can be reduced or sometimes eliminated by advance planning. It is also true that planning is sometimes incomplete, and that probate is the cleanup mechanism for property that planning did not reach. Neither of these facts makes probate a verdict.

Misunderstanding 4 — “Probate Is Always Bad”

Probate has reliable institutional features that, in some cases, are actually preferred. Among them:

- the court's protection against creditor claims that surface after the window closes,
- the court's adjudication of validity when the will or its execution is questioned,
- the court's supervision of distributions to minors and incapacitated beneficiaries,
- the court's protection of the executor against later claims of breach when proper notice and accounting were given.

Families who avoid probate at all costs sometimes give up these protections without realizing it. A trust avoids probate. It also avoids the creditor-window cutoff that probate provides. A trust trustee can be sued for distributions five years after the closing. An executor of a properly closed probate cannot. There are real tradeoffs here, and the right answer depends on the family's circumstances, not on a categorical preference.

Misunderstanding 5 — "The Court Will Make It Fair"

The court will make it lawful. The court does not have a mandate to make it fair, and most probate courts will tell you so directly.

The will may distribute ninety percent to one child and ten percent to another. The court will enforce that. It is not the court's role to override testamentary intent on the basis of a beneficiary's sense of fairness. A beneficiary who believes the unequal distribution reflects undue influence or lack of capacity may contest the will, with the burdens described in Chapter 7. Absent such a contest, the will controls.

"Fair" and "lawful" are usually compatible in well-drafted estate plans. They are not the same word.

Misunderstanding 6 — "The Estate Lawyer Represents the Family"

The estate's lawyer represents the executor, in the executor's capacity as personal representative of the estate. The lawyer does not represent the beneficiaries. The lawyer does not represent the family as a unit. Beneficiaries who believe the estate's lawyer is their lawyer often share information, ask questions, and rely on advice that the lawyer is not actually authorized to give.

If a beneficiary needs counsel, the beneficiary should hire their own. The estate's lawyer can be perfectly cordial and helpful without being the beneficiary's representative. The distinction matters most when conflict arises — the moment when beneficiaries discover that the estate's lawyer cannot, and will not, advocate on their behalf.

Misunderstanding 7 — "Probate Costs Half the Estate"

Probate costs vary. In most ordinary estates, total costs (court fees, attorney fees, executor fees, appraisal fees, accounting fees) fall in the range of three to seven percent of the gross estate. Larger estates, where statutory percentages are tiered, can pay less in percentage terms but more in absolute dollars.

The "probate costs half the estate" figure is essentially never accurate as a baseline. It can become accurate in catastrophic cases — a contested will, a litigated removal, multi-state ancillary proceedings, a tax controversy. In the ordinary case, however, the cost is closer to a real-estate commission than to a casualty loss.

Table 8.1

Estate type	Typical total cost	As % of gross estate
Small estate (affidavit procedure)	$200–$1,500	0.1–1%
Simple estate, will, no real property	$3,000–$8,000	1–4%
Simple estate, will, with real property	$5,000–$15,000	2–5%
Complex estate, business interests	$15,000–$60,000	2–6%
Estate-tax-return required	$25,000–$150,000+	1–3%
Contested will (full litigation)	$80,000–$500,000+	5–25%

Approximate probate cost ranges (verify with current local figures).

Misunderstanding 8 — "The Estate Will Pay Off the Mortgage"

Mortgages survive death. They run with the property, secured by the house, and they continue to require monthly payments. The estate is not automatically responsible for paying off the mortgage. The beneficiary who inherits the house typically inherits the mortgage as well, in some form.

There are nuances. Federally guaranteed mortgages have due-on-sale clauses that may or may not apply when title passes by inheritance (the Garn-St. Germain Depository Institutions Act provides protection in many residential cases). State law treats some transfers more leniently than others. But the default expectation should be: the mortgage continues. Plan for that.

Misunderstanding 9 — "No Will Means the State Takes Everything"

Dying without a will is called dying intestate. It does not mean the state confiscates the estate. It means the state's intestate-succession statute determines who takes.

Intestate succession typically goes to the nearest living relatives in a defined order: spouse, then children, then parents, then siblings, then more distant relatives. The state takes (this is called escheat) only when there are no living relatives within the statute's reach — a circumstance that is rare in practice.

The real cost of dying intestate is not that the state takes the money. The real cost is that the deceased's preferences are irrelevant. A long-time partner not formally married does not inherit. A favorite charity does not receive a bequest. A disinherited family member who would have been disinherited under a will receives a share. The intestate-succession statute is a default rule. It is rarely the rule a particular family would have chosen.

Misunderstanding 10 — "Probate Is Private"

Probate is, with very few exceptions, public. The will, once filed, becomes a public record. The inventory, in many states, is public. The accounting can be inspected. Anyone with a curiosity and a computer terminal at the courthouse can usually see the broad outlines of an estate's contents and disposition.

For most families this does not matter. For some — wealthy families, public figures, families with particular reasons for confidentiality — it matters considerably. A trust, by contrast, is a private instrument and is not filed publicly in most cases. The choice between a will-driven and a trust-driven plan is, in part, a choice about privacy.

> **KEY POINT**
>
> The misunderstandings about probate are not signs of negligence. They are signs that the system is taught poorly. Correcting them is the work of the first half of any honest conversation about estate planning.

Why These Beliefs Persist

It is worth pausing on why these misunderstandings are so durable. Three reasons stand out:

First, probate happens once or twice in most peoples' lives — once for a parent, perhaps once more for a spouse. There is no opportunity to develop the kind of practical familiarity that corrects misconceptions in domains adults engage with regularly, like buying houses or filing taxes.

Second, the marketing of competing products — "avoid probate at all costs" being the headline — is loud and consistent. Few are paid to describe probate accurately. Many are paid to describe it as a calamity from which their product offers escape.

What This Looks Like in Practice

A retired schoolteacher in her sixties asks her financial advisor whether she should set up a trust. She has been told, repeatedly, that her will alone will not avoid probate. She has also been told — by a different source — that her estate will be eaten alive by probate fees. She is afraid. She wants to act.

Her advisor, who is good at this, slows the conversation down. He asks her what she actually owns. She owns a house jointly with her husband (who is alive). She owns a small brokerage account with her husband as TOD beneficiary. She has a 401(k) with her husband as primary beneficiary and her two children as contingent beneficiaries. She has a checking account in her individual name with about six thousand dollars in it.

Her advisor walks her through what would happen if she died tomorrow. The house would pass to her husband by survivorship. The brokerage account would pass to her husband by TOD. The 401(k) would pass to her husband by beneficiary designation. The checking account would be the only probate asset, and at six thousand dollars it would clear the small-estate threshold in her state. There would be no full probate. There would be no probate fees in the catastrophic sense she had feared. The total cost would be a one-page affidavit and a filing fee.

She does not need a trust. She needs to update her checking account to add a payable-on-death designation to her husband, which she does the next morning at her bank. The fifteen-minute conversation has saved her several thousand dollars in unnecessary trust drafting and several years of anxiety. She had been planning around a misunderstanding.

This is what most probate misunderstandings look like in practice. The fear is real. The action it produces is often wrong. The corrective conversation is brief, free, and available — when the family asks the right person.

Third, the law is genuinely state-specific. A friend's experience in Florida is informative, but it may be misleading in California. Generalized advice picked up across state lines almost always introduces error.

Notes on Practice

A pattern worth naming directly: the families that arrive at estate planning carrying the fewest misconceptions are not the wealthiest. They are the ones whose own previous experience with probate — administering a parent's estate, or a sibling's, or an aunt's — has corrected the misconceptions the surrounding culture had supplied.

First-generation experience is the most reliable corrective. An adult child who has spent a year as executor of a parent's estate emerges from that year with a calibrated, realistic sense of what probate is and is not. They have watched the creditor window run. They have filed the inventory. They have paid the closing costs. The misconceptions that previously felt urgent now look implausible to them. The estate plan they make for themselves a few years later is almost always more measured than the plan they would have made before.

This suggests an unflattering implication for the marketing-driven side of the estate-planning industry: the people most exposed to its messaging are the people who have not yet had personal experience to test it against. Once they have that experience, the marketing tends to lose its grip. A book like this one is, in a small way, a substitute for that experience — a way of borrowing other people's calibration before having to acquire one's own.

Probate is a process, not a verdict. Approached with accurate expectations, it is one of the more reliable institutions in American private law.

KEY POINT

Most planning around probate begins with a misunderstanding. The first hour of any honest estate-planning conversation is spent correcting beliefs that are widely held and incorrect. The plans that follow that hour are almost always different — and better — than the plans that would have been built on the original assumptions.

What This Chapter Has Said

Ten widely held beliefs about probate consistently produce avoidable conflict and unnecessary expense. The will does not avoid probate. The executor does not control everything. Probate does not mean failure. Probate is not always bad. The court does not make it fair. The estate's lawyer does not represent the family. Probate does not cost half the estate. The estate does not pay off the mortgage by default. Dying intestate does not give the property to the state. Probate is not private. Each of these beliefs is sufficiently common that careful planners proactively address all of them with their clients before any document is signed.

CHAPTER 9

Why Probate Feels Personal

Chapter at a Glance

- Why probate feels personal even when none of the procedure is meant to be.
- The two calendars — legal and emotional — that run simultaneously and disagree.
- Where the mismatch becomes visible in concrete moments of the administration.
- Why communication is the single highest-leverage intervention available to the executor.
- Why family fractures that pre-existed the death surface during probate, and what to do about them.

Probate happens during grief.

That sentence, on its own, accounts for more of probate's reputation than any procedural fact in the entire process. Estate administration is asked to operate, by the law, in the moments and months when the family is least equipped to operate at all. Legal timelines collide with emotional timelines. Procedures designed for consistency are experienced as cold. Communications written in the careful language of fiduciary practice are read by people who are still trying to absorb what has happened.

This mismatch is rarely named directly in the literature. It deserves to be.

Two Calendars, Running at Once

Every estate runs on two calendars simultaneously. The legal calendar is what we have described in this book — petition, notice, creditor window, inventory, tax filings, distribution, closing. It is measured in months. It is structured. Its dates do not move.

The emotional calendar is something else entirely. Grief is non-linear. It does not converge on a steady-state by month seven. It is louder in some months than others. Birthdays trigger it. Holidays trigger it. The first time the executor enters the deceased's house and sees the unread mail on the counter triggers it. The first time the brokerage statement arrives in the deceased's name with the words Estate of preceding it triggers it. None of these moments is on the legal calendar. All of them are real.

Families that understand both calendars exist tend to navigate probate without becoming estranged. Families that try to operate on one calendar — either pretending grief is not present, or refusing to engage with the legal procedure until grief has resolved — are the ones that come apart.

Where the Mismatch Becomes Visible

The mismatch becomes visible at predictable moments in the administration:

1. **Bank-account freeze.** The deceased's account is frozen the day after the bank is notified. Direct deposits stop. Auto-pays continue or fail. The surviving spouse, who used the joint account for everything, discovers that what was joint may not have been as joint as they thought.
2. **Sorting personal belongings.** Adult children are asked to come together to divide tangible personal property. The conversations they expected to have about their mother's life become conversations about her necklace.
3. **Reading the will.** The will distributes assets in proportions that, on hearing them, surprise one or more beneficiaries. The surprise is rarely mathematical. It is interpretive — what did the parent mean by this — and the answer cannot be retrieved.
4. **Selling the house.** The house in which the family was raised goes on the market. Even when all beneficiaries agreed to the sale, the day the sign goes up in the yard is harder than expected.
5. **Closing the estate.** The final accounting arrives. The check is written. The estate's bank account is closed. The deceased's name disappears from another set of records. The administrative ending arrives without ceremony — and

that, too, can be hard.

Each of these moments is a procedural step. Each is also a small act of letting go. The executor and the family who recognize this tend to handle each moment with more patience than they otherwise would.

Why Communication Matters More Than People Expect

If we had to identify the single intervention most likely to make a probate administration go smoothly across the family, it would not be choice of counsel, choice of jurisdiction, choice of executor, or even sophistication of the underlying estate plan.

It would be communication.

Specifically: a regular, honest, written update from the executor to all beneficiaries explaining what has happened in the past month, what is happening now, what is expected next, and why the next thing has not happened yet. Even when the update is brief — even when the update is, in substance, “the creditor window is still open and we are waiting” — its presence prevents almost the entire category of beneficiary anxiety that produces objections, removal petitions, and contested closings.

Beneficiaries who receive monthly updates rarely sue executors. Beneficiaries who hear nothing for six months sometimes do.

REFLECTION

The least expensive risk-reduction tool in probate is a one-page email at the end of every month, written by the executor, saying what happened. The cost is twenty minutes. The benefit is incalculable.

Why the Executor Becomes the Lightning Rod

Family tension during probate often concentrates on the executor. The executor is visible. The executor is making decisions. The executor is the one telling beneficiaries that they cannot have what they want, when they want it. A family that was, before the death, a network of equals becomes, in the months of administration, a structure with one decision-maker at the center.

This is not a flaw in the executor. It is a feature of the role.

Executors who understand this in advance tend to handle the pressure with grace. They expect to be asked questions they cannot fully answer. They expect to be the messenger of news that is not their fault. They expect their objectivity to be challenged. They do the role anyway.

Executors who do not understand this often take the pressure personally. They become defensive, then withdrawn, then resentful. The administration suffers. The family relationships suffer more.

When the Family Is Already Fractured

Probate is a poor venue for healing existing family fractures. It is also a remarkably common venue for them to surface.

Adult siblings who have not spoken since high school find themselves co-beneficiaries of the same estate. A child who left the family twenty years ago returns. A second spouse and the deceased's children from a prior marriage discover they are sharing a distribution that neither thought they would have to share. Old favoritism, real or imagined, comes back into view through the lens of who got what in the will.

The mistake families make in these situations is to treat the probate proceeding as the venue for resolving the underlying fracture. It is not. It is a venue for resolving the orderly transfer of property. The fracture, if it can be resolved, will have to be resolved separately.

Executors handling fractured families serve everyone best by drawing the line clearly: the estate's job is to administer the deceased's directions, not to repair what the deceased's life did not repair.

Why Compassion Is Not the Court's Job

We have said it before, and it bears saying again. The probate court is not the right institution to extend compassion to a family in grief. The court's compassion, if we can call it that, is delivered through the steady, predictable, indifferent operation of procedure. The judge does not condole with the family. The judge applies the statute.

What looks cold in the moment is, on a longer view, a kind of respect. The court is treating the deceased's preferences as binding. It is treating the family's relationships as private. It is taking no position on which beneficiary deserves more or less. It is doing exactly what an institution is supposed to do when asked to administer something across a divided family: nothing extra.

What This Chapter Has Said

Probate feels personal because it is administered during a personal moment. The legal procedure cannot adjust to that moment, and it should not try. What can adjust — what must adjust, if the family is to come through the process intact — is the family's understanding of what the procedure is and is not trying to do.

What This Looks Like in Practice

A widow in her seventies is administering her husband's estate. Her two adult sons have come home for the funeral and stayed for several days. The sons are not close to each other. One lives nearby and has been involved in the parents' lives for two decades. The other lives across the country and has visited rarely.

On the morning of the third day, while sorting through the deceased's clothes and personal items, the two sons reach a small disagreement about a watch. The watch belonged to the deceased's father — the sons' grandfather — and had been intended, in some indistinct family understanding, for the elder son. The will did not specifically mention the watch. The personal-property memorandum, if there ever was one, is not in the file. The younger son believes he has as much claim to the watch as his brother.

The mother, watching this, recognizes immediately what is happening. The watch is not the disagreement. The watch is the occasion. Twenty years of accumulated resentment about who was present and who was not, who carried the parents' aging years and who did not, has now found a small, valuable object on which to land.

She does the right thing. She steps back and lets the brothers argue. She does not try to mediate. She does not try to resolve. After about forty minutes, the brothers run out of things to say.

They agree, awkwardly, that the elder son will take the watch, and that the younger son will choose another item of comparable family significance. The disagreement, which had felt structural, deflates the moment they have finished saying what they actually wanted to say.

This is what probate looks like at its most personal. The procedure is irrelevant in the moment. The legal calendar is irrelevant in the moment. What matters is two adult children who have not had the conversation they needed to have, and an object of memory that has finally given them an excuse to have it. The watch was never the question.

The procedure is trying to transfer ownership lawfully.

Notes on Practice

An observation that practitioners share but that rarely appears in written treatments: probate experiences differ sharply between families that mourn together and families that mourn separately.

Families that come together for the funeral, sit together afterward, and continue to communicate weekly through the administration tend to close estates with their relationships improved rather than damaged. The shared experience produces a kind of forced intimacy that, handled well, becomes one of the lasting positive byproducts of the death.

Families that disperse immediately after the funeral and communicate primarily through the executor's monthly updates tend to close estates in roughly the same condition the relationships were in before the death. The administration neither helps nor hurts them, particularly.

Families that were already fractured before the death and do not engage with each other during the administration tend to close estates with the fractures wider than before. Probate is not the cause; it is the occasion. The death merely creates the next round of the conflict that was already underway.

Families considering whether to invest in active communication during probate should weigh which of the three patterns describes them. Communication helps the second pattern most, prevents the third pattern from worsening, and makes the first pattern even better. It is rarely wasted effort.

The family will have to do the rest.

Figure 9.1

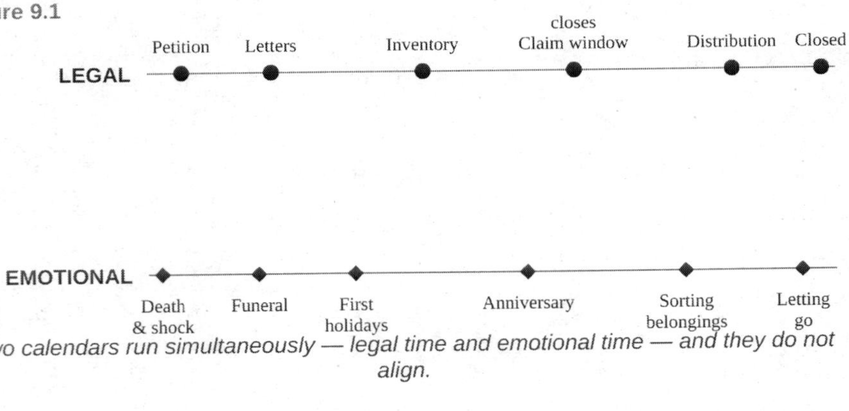

Two calendars run simultaneously — legal time and emotional time — and they do not align.

> **KEY POINT**
>
> A monthly written update from the executor to all beneficiaries is the single least expensive, highest-yield intervention in probate. It costs twenty minutes per month and it prevents almost the entire category of beneficiary anxiety that otherwise produces objections, removal petitions, and contested closings.

What This Chapter Has Said

Probate happens during grief, on a calendar that does not match the calendar of grief. The mismatch produces almost every complaint families ever raise. The administration runs on legal time; the family lives on emotional time. The two calendars are not made to align, but they can be acknowledged and, with care, navigated together. Communication is the single highest-leverage tool an executor has. Family fractures that pre-existed the death surface during probate; the cleanest response is to draw the line clearly between what the estate is for (orderly transfer of property) and what it is not for (repair of relationships).

PART VI

RESOLUTION AND LEGACY

How probate ends, and what comes after.

CHAPTER 10

What Happens When Probate Ends

Chapter at a Glance

- How probate ends, in three sequential steps that must all be complete.
- What the closing of an estate actually looks like in practice.
- What every beneficiary should receive at closing — five specific items.
- What does not survive the closing, and what does.
- Why the quietness of the ending is the institution working as designed.

Probate ends quietly. There is no ceremony, no announcement. After months — sometimes years — of paperwork, hearings, accountings, and deliberations, the estate closes with a brief court order, a final wire transfer or set of distribution checks, and a single page in a court file. The next morning, no one in particular notices that anything has changed.

And yet, the change is total. Title to property has shifted. Authority that was vested in a personal representative has dissolved. The deceased's name has been removed from one ledger after another. The estate, which existed as a legal entity for the duration of the administration, simply ceases to be.

How Probate Actually Ends

Three things, in sequence, must happen before an estate is closed:

1. **Debts and claims are resolved.** Every valid creditor claim has been paid or compromised. Rejected claims have been litigated to conclusion or have lapsed. Tax returns have been filed and any required closing letters obtained. Estate-tax matters, if applicable, have been cleared.

2. **Court requirements are satisfied.** The executor has filed the final accounting, given notice to the beneficiaries, and either obtained their written consent to the accounting or had a hearing on any objections. The court has reviewed the accounting and approved it.

3. **Assets are legally transferred.** The remaining property has been distributed to the beneficiaries — by cash distribution, by retitling of real estate, by transfer of brokerage assets, by delivery of tangible personal property. The executor has obtained and filed receipts from the beneficiaries acknowledging their respective shares.

When all three steps are complete, the executor petitions for discharge. The court, having found the executor has performed the duties of office, releases the executor from further responsibility. The bond, if any, is exonerated. The estate is closed.

What Closing Actually Looks Like

Closing rarely produces a single dramatic moment. Instead, it is a set of small, accumulating completions:

- the final estate-account check is written and the account is closed,
- the deeds transferring real estate from the estate to the named beneficiaries are recorded with the county,
- the brokerage account is transferred or distributed and the estate's account is closed,
- the safe-deposit box is emptied and the contents distributed,
- the household goods have been distributed or sold,
- the personal effects (photographs, papers, mementos) have been allocated,
- the executor receives the court's order of discharge and files it in the estate folder,
- the executor delivers a final letter to the beneficiaries — closing report, summary of distributions, copies of court orders.

After this, the executor's role ends. The beneficiaries hold their distributions in their own names. The estate, as a separate legal entity, is gone.

What the Beneficiary Should Receive at Closing

A well-run estate produces, at closing, a small file for each beneficiary containing:

1. **A copy of the final accounting.** Every dollar that came in. Every dollar that went out. The running balance. The final disposition.
2. **Copies of the court orders.** Approval of the accounting. Authorization of distribution. Discharge of the executor.
3. **A receipt for the distribution received.** The beneficiary's signed acknowledgment of what they received and that the estate's obligations to them are discharged.
4. **Tax documents related to the distribution.** K-1 schedules from the estate's final tax return showing any income or distributions reportable on the beneficiary's personal return.
5. **Asset-specific documents where applicable.** Recorded deeds for real property received. Stock-transfer confirmations. Title-transfer paperwork for vehicles. The items the beneficiary will need to actually use or sell what they have inherited.

Beneficiaries who receive a clean closing file are in a position to manage their inheritance from day one. Beneficiaries who do not — who receive a check and nothing else — sometimes spend years trying to reconstruct basic information about what they received, and what tax basis attaches to it, and what they can or cannot do with it.

What Does Not Survive Closing

Certain things end at closing that beneficiaries sometimes expect to continue:

- the executor's authority to act for the estate (it dissolves),
- the estate's tax-identification number (it can no longer be used after closing year),
- the estate's right to bring or defend lawsuits in its own name,
- the protection of the probate court's creditor-claim cutoff (it survives, but only against creditors who were properly noticed; new claims that emerge against beneficiaries personally must be addressed by the beneficiaries personally),
- the executor's compensation entitlement (any remaining unpaid fee must be claimed before closing).

Each of these endings is intentional. The institution of probate is designed to have a definite stop. The deceased's affairs cannot remain in administrative suspension forever. The orderly close is the final, and in some ways the most important, function of the system.

What Survives Closing

Several things do persist beyond the closing of an estate:

1. **Trusts that the will established.** Many wills establish testamentary trusts — for minor children, for special-needs beneficiaries, for spousal-protection purposes — that come into existence at the close of probate and continue independently. The successor trustee takes over. The terms of the trust govern from that point forward.
2. **Beneficiaries' tax obligations.** Inherited IRAs require withdrawal under the post-2020 ten-year rule (with some exceptions). Inherited brokerage assets carry stepped-up basis. Inherited real estate has a new basis. These are matters the beneficiary will engage with for years.
3. **Subsequent claims against beneficiaries.** If a creditor was not noticed because the executor did not know about the debt, and the creditor surfaces after closing, the creditor may sometimes pursue the beneficiaries directly for the value of what they received. The protection that probate's creditor-claim cutoff provides runs against the estate. It does not always run against the beneficiaries.
4. **The executor's potential liability.** The executor's discharge by the court protects against most claims of

breach. It does not protect against fraud, willful misconduct, or claims that were unknown at closing. Executors who run a clean administration are at minimal risk. Executors who do not are sometimes pursued years after the estate has closed.

The Quiet Conclusion

When the file is closed and the discharge order is signed, the estate is, in a real sense, finished. The deceased's affairs have been wound up. The property has reached the people entitled to receive it. The court has approved what was done.

What remains is what the deceased actually intended to leave: the property itself, in the hands of the named beneficiaries, free of the deceased's name and free of the apparatus that transferred it. The institution of probate has done what it was designed to do. It has stepped back.

Probate is not designed to comfort families. It is designed to transfer ownership lawfully.

Once that purpose is understood, probate becomes less frightening — not because it disappears, but because it becomes predictable. Predictable is the most valuable thing an institution can be at the moments when families have the least capacity to handle surprise.

What This Looks Like in Practice

An estate that opened in early March closes in late February of the following year. The executor, the deceased's daughter, receives the order discharging her in the morning mail. She places it in the binder of estate documents she has kept since week one. The binder, which began as a stack of unsorted papers, is now organized, indexed, complete. It includes the death certificate, the will, the petition, the order of appointment, the Letters Testamentary, the inventory, the notice publications, the creditor claims (allowed and rejected), the tax filings, the final accounting, the distribution receipts, and now the order of discharge.

She closes the binder. She sets it on the shelf next to her father's old binders — the ones he kept of his own affairs, the ones she found in his study the first week. The shelf now holds two binders that summarize a life: his, and the year of administering what he left behind.

There is no party. There is no announcement. The estate's bank account closed last week. The brokerage account transferred its remaining balance two days ago. The deeds to the house and the rental property are recorded in the names of the new beneficiaries. The children — herself, her sister, her brother — each received their share. Each signed the receipt. Each filed their own copies.

She makes herself a cup of coffee. She sits down at her own kitchen table. The estate, which had occupied a substantial share of her thinking for fourteen months, is closed. Her father is still gone. The grief is still its own ongoing thing. But the legal apparatus is finished. The institution of probate has done what it was built to do, and it has stepped back.

What remains is what her father intended to leave: the property, in the hands of the people he meant to receive it, free of the apparatus that transferred it. That is the ending. It is, in nearly every case, this quiet.

This book does not remove probate.

Notes on Practice

Two final practical observations close this chapter.

The first concerns what the executor should do with the estate's records after closing. State laws vary, but as a general rule the executor should retain a complete copy of the estate file for at least seven years after closing. The tax-statute periods extend that long; subsequent claims, while rare, can extend longer still. The cleanest practice is to digitize the entire file at closing — every petition, every order, every receipt, every tax return — and keep the original binder for the same period. Beneficiaries, advisors, and successor counsel sometimes need access years later.

The second concerns the closing letter from the executor to the beneficiaries. This letter is not legally required. It is, however, one of the most appreciated single documents in the entire administration. It thanks the beneficiaries for their patience, summarizes what was administered and how, acknowledges any difficult moments, and closes the executor's role with grace. Beneficiaries who receive such a letter remember it for decades. Beneficiaries who do not — who receive only a check and an accounting — sometimes recall the closing as cold even when the rest of the administration was handled well. The cost is twenty minutes. The benefit is the kind that does not show up on any balance sheet.

It removes confusion.

Figure 10.1

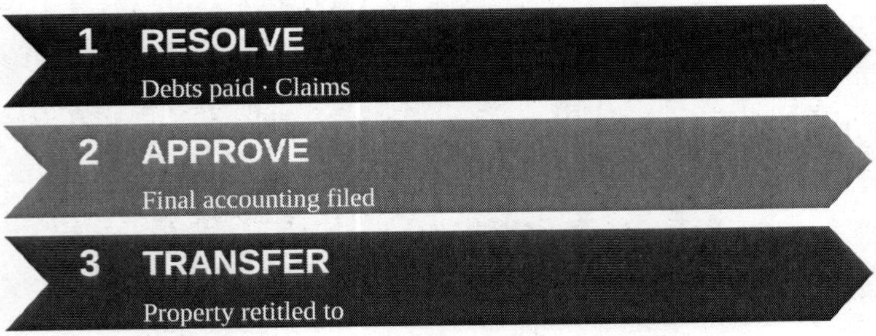

The closing sequence — three sequential phases that complete the estate.

KEY POINT

Probate ends quietly. There is no ceremony. The court's order discharging the executor is a single page filed in a binder. And yet the change is total: title has shifted, authority has dissolved, and the estate as a legal entity is gone. The institution has done what it was built to do.

What This Chapter Has Said

Probate ends through three sequential steps: resolution of debts and claims, satisfaction of court requirements, and legal transfer of the remaining property. The closing produces specific deliverables for each beneficiary. Some obligations survive the closing — testamentary trusts continue, beneficiaries' tax obligations attach, the executor's fiduciary duty extends in narrow circumstances — but most categories of subsequent claim are barred. The institution's definite stop is part of its design. Predictability is the most valuable thing it offers, and predictability is the ending it provides.

CONCLUSION

The Quiet Power of Understanding the Process

◆

We have come a long way, and it is worth pausing to take stock of what the journey has produced.

We began with the structural fact that a probate court is the system that creates legal authority to act for the estate of someone who has died. We moved through which assets require that authority and which transfer outside it. We treated the first thirty days of the administration, the role of the personal representative, the limits of the court, the calendar of the process, and the small set of pressure points where families consistently get into trouble. We named the misunderstandings that produce most of the avoidable conflict, and we treated the human side of probate — the mismatch between legal time and the time of grief, the way the executor becomes a lightning rod, the way old fractures surface in moments of administrative pressure. We closed with the quiet conclusion of an estate at the end of its work.

If the book has done its job, three convictions should now be available to you that may not have been available before.

First, that probate is a process — not a verdict, not a punishment, not a sign of failure on the part of the deceased or the family. It is the institutional response to a recurring structural problem. Like all institutions, it can be navigated well or badly. The difference is rarely about wealth and almost always about understanding.

Second, that the variables you can actually control matter more than the variables you cannot. You cannot control the creditor-claim window. You cannot accelerate the court's calendar. You cannot change the statute under which the will is administered. What you can do — by attention to titling during life, by clear drafting, by thoughtful selection of executor, by orderly communication with beneficiaries during administration — has, in aggregate, more impact on the family's experience than every uncontrollable variable combined.

Third, that the same calm that the court extends to the procedure is available to the family. The court treats the matter as routine because, on its long view, the matter is routine. Tens of millions of estates have been administered. The structure works. The calendar works. The closing works. A family that approaches the process with the same calm — informed by the procedure, patient with the calendar, kind to the executor — almost always closes the chapter intact.

Probate is not the most glamorous institution in private American law. It is, however, one of the most reliable. For the family that arrives at it informed, it is a structure that does what it is supposed to do, in the time it is supposed to take, with a predictable result at the end.

That is the value of understanding it before it arrives.

And that is the work this book set out to do.

— A. Perkins

AVOY Publishing

Spring 2026

CHAPTER 11

When Probate Meets a Trust

Chapter at a Glance

- The standard four-element modern estate plan: trust, pour-over will, beneficiary designations, joint titling.
- How the four mechanisms operate in parallel after death.
- The pour-over will explained — what it does, what it doesn't, and why it still requires probate.
- The funding gap — the single most common failure in modern estate planning.
- How the estate's tax life and the trust's tax life run as two separate Form 1041 returns post-death.
- Why lifetime funding discipline is the single highest-leverage habit in any trust-plus-will plan.

Most modern estate plans are not pure-probate plans. They are not pure-trust plans either. They are some combination of the two — a revocable trust as the principal vehicle, a will as the safety net, beneficiary designations on retirement and life-insurance accounts, and joint titling on the marital home. The result is that, when one of these settlors dies, three different mechanisms transfer property in parallel.

This chapter treats the interface between probate and the trust. It is not a chapter about how to set up a trust — that subject is the domain of the companion volume Trust Made Simple. It is about what happens when an estate has a trust and a probate administration running at the same time, and how the two interact.

The Standard Trust-Plus-Will Architecture

The most common modern estate plan has four elements:

1. **A revocable living trust** that holds the principal assets — the house, the brokerage account, business interests, and any real property in other states. The settlor is also the trustee during life and the primary beneficiary; a successor trustee takes over at death or incapacity.
2. **A pour-over will** as the safety net. Its principal function is to direct any asset that the settlor failed to transfer into the trust during life — a forgotten account, a vehicle bought late in life, a post-funding inheritance — into the trust at death. The pour-over will itself must be admitted to probate before it can operate, but it typically does so quickly because the residue of the estate is small.
3. **Beneficiary designations** on retirement accounts (IRAs, 401(k)s) and life insurance, naming individuals or — for special-needs or minor beneficiaries — the trust itself or a designated sub-trust.

4. **Joint titling** with right of survivorship, principally on the marital residence and joint bank accounts. Survivorship is the simplest non-probate transfer mechanism and the one most families default to without thinking about it.

When the first of two married settlors dies, all four mechanisms operate at once. The marital house transfers by survivorship in a few days. The retirement accounts pay to the named beneficiary in two to four weeks. The trust continues administration under the successor trustee — usually the surviving spouse — without skipping a beat. Only the small residue of individually titled assets goes through probate, and the pour-over will directs it back to the trust within a few months.

From the family's perspective, this looks like an estate that barely went through probate at all. From the law's perspective, it went through probate exactly the way the system was designed to handle estates that were planned in advance.

The Pour-Over Will, in Detail

The pour-over will is the most consequential, and most misunderstood, document in the standard trust plan.

Its name describes its function. Whatever assets remain in the deceased's individual name at death — assets that did not make it into the trust during life, that were not jointly titled, that did not have a beneficiary designation — are poured over into the trust by the will's directive. The trust then administers them under its existing terms.

Three things make the pour-over will important:

1. **It must be admitted to probate.** A pour-over will is still a will. It must be filed, the court must admit it, and a personal representative must be appointed even if the estate's probate residue is small. This is the minimum probate footprint for nearly every trust-plus-will estate.
2. **It only handles what the trust missed.** Assets already inside the trust pass under the trust agreement, not under the will. Assets with beneficiary designations pass under the contract with the custodian. Jointly titled assets pass by survivorship. The pour-over will is the catch-net for what is left.
3. **It does not modify the trust.** The pour-over will refers to the trust by name and date; it does not restate the trust's distributive provisions. If the settlor wants to change who takes, the change must be made in the trust, not in the pour-over will. Pour-over wills are intentionally short — typically two to four pages — for this reason.

The Funding Gap

The single most common failure in modern estate planning is not a drafting error. It is a funding gap. The settlor signed the trust, paid the lawyer, and then never got around to actually transferring all of the assets into the trust's name.

What this looks like: the deed to the house was retitled into the trust at signing, but the brokerage account was forgotten. Or the primary brokerage was retitled, but a smaller secondary account opened later was never funded. Or all the financial accounts were moved, but a vehicle bought five years after the trust was signed still sits in the settlor's individual name.

The funding gap is what the pour-over will is there to address. But the pour-over only operates after probate is opened — and probate, even a small one, takes months and consumes fees the family did not need to pay. The cleanest practice is to fund the trust completely during life and revisit funding annually. The Trust Funding Checklist in Trust Made Simple's Appendix A is a practical guide; the same discipline applies to any trust plan.

Table 11.1

Asset category	Probate path	Trust path
Trust-titled real estate	—	Successor trustee takes over.
Trust-titled brokerage	—	Successor trustee assumes.
Bank account in trust name	—	Trust controls.
Account left in individual name	Probate residue (pour-over)	—
Vehicle in individual name (late buy)	Probate residue	—
Retirement w/ beneficiary	—	Pays beneficiary directly.
Retirement payable to trust	—	Pays into trust by contract.
Life insurance w/ beneficiary	—	Pays beneficiary directly.
House jointly titled w/ spouse	—	Survivor takes by operation of law.
Tort claim arising at death	Probate (executor pursues)	—

What goes through probate when the deceased had a trust.

> **KEY POINT**
>
> A trust does not eliminate probate. It reduces the surface area where probate can attach, often to nearly zero. The remainder is what the pour-over will is for. A small probate residue is not a failure of the plan; it is the plan working as designed.

Tax Interface — The Estate's Income, the Trust's Income

After death, two separate income-tax-paying entities typically exist: the estate (administered by the executor) and the trust (administered by the successor trustee). Each files its own annual income-tax return — Form 1041 for the estate, the same Form 1041 for the trust. The two are coordinated but distinct.

Three timing matters arise from this:

- The estate's tax year. Executors typically elect a fiscal year that ends 11 months after death, which gives the family flexibility about which year's income falls on which beneficiary's personal return.
- The trust's tax year. Calendar year by default; cannot elect a fiscal year unless the trust is a qualified domestic trust or makes specific elections. The trust files for income earned by trust-titled assets after death.
- Coordination. Distributions from the estate to the trust during the estate's administration carry out the estate's distributable net income to the trust. Distributions from the trust to beneficiaries do the same for the trust's income. Careful coordination by the CPA between executor and trustee avoids double-taxation and missed deductions.

When the Trust Funds Late

An estate plan that funds the trust ON the death — by pour-over from probate — is a meaningfully weaker plan than one that funded the trust during life. The reasons:

1. **The pour-over passes through probate first.** Whatever goes through probate is exposed to creditor claims, court oversight, and the public record during the administration. Lifetime funding bypasses all of that.

2. **The probate creditor cutoff does not protect trust assets.** Creditors barred from claims against the estate at the close of probate may, in some jurisdictions, still pursue trust assets that received post-death pour-over funding within a longer statutory window. Lifetime funding completes the creditor-protection arithmetic.
3. **Probate fees apply to the residuary estate.** The pour-over residue is part of the gross estate for probate-fee purposes in jurisdictions that scale fees by estate size. Lifetime funding moves the same assets out of the gross-estate denominator.
4. **Privacy.** Anything that passes through the will (including the pour-over) becomes part of the public probate record. Trust assets transferred during life never enter that record.

None of these is catastrophic. All four are avoidable with a single afternoon of post-signing funding work and an annual ten-minute review of titles and beneficiary designations.

What This Looks Like in Practice

A widow in her late seventies signed a revocable trust eleven years before her death. At signing, she funded the house, the principal brokerage account, and three smaller bank accounts into the trust. Her IRA had her two adult children as primary beneficiaries; her life insurance had the same.

Over the next eleven years, she did three things her attorney would have wished she did differently. She bought a vacation condo in another state and titled it in her individual name. She opened a new high-yield savings account at a different bank without funding it into the trust. She sold the original brokerage account and rolled the proceeds into a new account at a different firm — but the new account was opened in her individual name, not the trust's.

When she died, her estate had three probate assets: the new brokerage account, the new savings account, and the out-of-state vacation condo. The principal probate ran in her home state for the brokerage and savings accounts and took eleven months. An ancillary probate ran in the second state for the condo and took an additional five months. The pour-over will directed all three assets back into the trust at the close of each proceeding.

Her family eventually received exactly what she intended. But the process took sixteen months instead of the four it would have taken if she had retitled those three assets during life. The estate paid roughly $35,000 in fees and ancillary costs that would not have been incurred. The family also discovered, during the ancillary proceeding, that the second-state probate court treated the brokerage account as part of the gross estate for fee purposes — a result her attorney had not anticipated and her advisor had not flagged.

The pour-over will did exactly what it was supposed to do. The trust did exactly what it was supposed to do. The settlor's lifetime funding discipline did not match the plan's design — and the cost was sixteen months, $35,000, and a small but real amount of family confusion. None of which was the plan's fault. All of which was preventable.

Notes on Practice

Three practical observations follow from the foregoing.

First, an annual review of titles and beneficiary designations is the most cost-effective single discipline in estate-plan maintenance. Schedule it on the same day each year — the settlor's birthday is a common choice — and walk through every asset acquired or sold in the prior twelve months.

Second, when retitling is administratively burdensome — for example, an out-of-state property whose retitling requires engaging counsel in that state — consider transfer-on-death deeds where the second state recognizes them. The cost is typically a few hundred dollars; the savings at death are in the tens of thousands.

Third, the trust's named successor trustee should be informed, in writing, that they have been named — and should be given a copy of the trust agreement during the settlor's lifetime. Successor trustees who first see the trust at the moment they have to administer it operate at a meaningful disadvantage.

Figure 11.1

REVOCABLE TRUST

Holds principal assets — house, brokerage, business interests. Successor trustee continues.

OUTSIDE PROBATE

POUR-OVER WILL

Catches anything left in individual name. Passes to trust at close of probate.

THROUGH PROBATE

BENEFICIARY DESIGNATIONS

IRAs, 401(k)s, life insurance. Pay named beneficiary directly by contract with custodian.

OUTSIDE PROBATE

JOINT TITLING

Marital home, joint accounts. Survivor takes by operation of law — no court involvement.

OUTSIDE PROBATE

The standard trust-plus-will architecture — four parallel transfer mechanisms operating at death.

REFLECTION

A trust without funding is a binder on a shelf. Funding without a trust is just careful titling. The two together — in disciplined combination, maintained over a lifetime — are what actually move property quietly across generations. The tools are well-documented. The discipline is the rare part.

What This Chapter Has Said

Most modern estates pass through some combination of trust, pour-over will, beneficiary designations, and joint titling. The interfaces between them are well-defined but require attention. The pour-over will is the safety net; the trust is the principal vehicle; both file separate income-tax returns post-death. The single most common failure is the funding gap — assets the settlor failed to retitle during life. Lifetime funding discipline is what makes the rest of the plan work as designed. The chapter does not duplicate the trust treatment in the companion volume Trust Made Simple; readers seeking a deeper treatment of trusts as instruments should consult that volume.

CHAPTER 12

Special Situations — When Probate Becomes Unusual

Chapter at a Glance

- Blended families — why they produce the most contested probate cases, and the four drafting devices that defuse them.
- Multi-state real property — why ancillary probate is expensive, and how trusts and TOD deeds avoid it.
- Minor beneficiaries — UTMA custodianship, testamentary trusts, and court-supervised guardianship of the estate.
- Beneficiaries with disabilities — special-needs trusts, pooled trusts, and disclaimers that preserve benefit eligibility.
- Digital assets — RUFADAA, cryptocurrency self-custody, and the platforms' in-app post-death tools.
- Missing original wills, holographic instruments, and the path forward when a will cannot be found.
- Insolvent estates — what creditors can reach, what they cannot, and why family is not personally liable.

Most probate cases follow the textbook arc. A small minority do not. This chapter treats the small minority — the situations in which the standard procedure either does not apply or applies in modified form. Each of these situations is uncommon individually; in aggregate, they account for a meaningful share of the cases practitioners describe as difficult.

Blended Families

A blended family in this context is one in which a deceased person leaves both a current spouse and children from a prior marriage or relationship. Blended-family estates are the single most common source of contested probate in the United States.

The structural problem is straightforward. A typical estate plan distributes outright to the surviving spouse — on the assumption that the spouse will, in time, leave what remains to the children. In a blended family, this assumption breaks. The surviving spouse's preferences and the deceased spouse's children may differ. Without specific drafting, the children of the first marriage may receive nothing.

Several drafting devices address this:

- QTIP trusts (Qualified Terminable Interest Property). The surviving spouse receives lifetime income; the principal passes at the surviving spouse's death to beneficiaries the deceased spouse named (typically the children of the first marriage).

- Marital trusts with mandatory remainder beneficiaries. The trust holds the marital share; the surviving spouse benefits during life; the named remainder beneficiaries take at the surviving spouse's death.
- Direct bequests to children at first death. A specific share — say, twenty-five percent — passes outright to the children of the first marriage, with the remainder going to the surviving spouse. Avoids ambiguity but reduces the surviving spouse's standard of living.
- Insurance-funded children's bequests. A life-insurance policy on the deceased spouse, payable to the children of the first marriage, replaces the value that would otherwise have gone to them.

Probate courts adjudicate blended-family disputes more often than any other category. The settlor's clearest signal of intent — through specific bequests, trust structures, or both — is the only reliable defense against the litigation that otherwise consumes both the estate and the family relationships.

Multi-State Real Property

When a deceased person owned real property in a state other than their state of domicile, the second state's probate jurisdiction must run a separate ancillary proceeding to transfer that property. We treat the procedural mechanics in Appendix N. Two practical observations belong here.

The ancillary proceeding adds, on average, four to nine months to the principal administration and ten to twenty thousand dollars in additional fees. The additional time cannot be compressed; the additional cost can usually be sharply reduced by avoiding the ancillary altogether. Three options for doing so:

1. **Title the property in a revocable trust.** The trust holds the asset; no probate of any kind is required at death. This is the most reliable option and the one most consistent with modern estate-planning practice.
2. **Use a transfer-on-death deed where state law allows.** Approximately half of U.S. states recognize TOD deeds for real property. Where they do, the deed transfers the property automatically at death without any court involvement. The cost of recording is a few hundred dollars; the savings are in the thousands.
3. **Hold the property through a single-member LLC owned by the trust.** Particularly for income-producing property in the second state, the LLC can simplify both lifetime management and the death transfer. The LLC's annual cost (state filing fee, registered-agent fee) typically pays for itself.

Estates with Minor Beneficiaries

When a beneficiary of an estate is a minor (under age eighteen or twenty-one, depending on state), the minor cannot legally receive distributions in their own name. Three mechanisms address this, in increasing order of formality:

1. **UTMA/UGMA custodianship.** The Uniform Transfers to Minors Act and the older Uniform Gifts to Minors Act allow distributions to be held by a named adult custodian until the minor reaches majority. Simple and inexpensive; the custodian is accountable to the minor at majority. Best for modest-value distributions.
2. **Testamentary trust.** The will (or, more commonly, the trust agreement) creates a sub-trust for the minor that holds the distribution until a specified age — often twenty-five or thirty. The trustee manages investments and authorized distributions. Best for meaningful-value distributions.
3. **Court-supervised guardianship of the estate.** If neither of the above is provided in the estate plan, the court may appoint a guardian of the minor's estate to manage the distribution until majority. The guardianship is its own annual proceeding with its own accounting requirements. The most expensive of the three; usually a result of incomplete estate planning.

Beneficiaries with Disabilities

A beneficiary receiving means-tested public benefits — Supplemental Security Income, Medicaid, certain housing assistance programs — can lose those benefits if they receive an outright distribution from the estate. The distribution counts as a resource for eligibility purposes.

Three mechanisms preserve benefit eligibility while still providing for the beneficiary:

- Special-needs trusts (SNT). The estate's distribution funds an SNT for the beneficiary; the trust supplements rather than replaces benefits; the principal is not a countable resource for eligibility.
- Pooled trusts. A non-profit organization pools special-needs trusts for multiple beneficiaries; lower setup cost than a stand-alone SNT; appropriate for smaller distributions.
- Disclaimers. A beneficiary on benefits may disclaim their share, allowing it to pass to a contingent beneficiary or back into a trust under qualified-disclaimer rules. Useful when the SNT was not pre-arranged.

Estate plans for families with a beneficiary on benefits should always include the SNT mechanism — drafted in advance, ready to receive the distribution at death. Retroactive special-needs planning at death is possible but harder.

Digital Assets

A growing share of the deceased's wealth and identity sits in digital form: brokerage accounts accessible only through online portals, cryptocurrency in self-custody wallets, social-media accounts, email archives, photo libraries, domain names, subscription services. The legal framework for transferring these is younger and less developed than for tangible property.

Three rules of practice apply:

1. **RUFADAA (Revised Uniform Fiduciary Access to Digital Assets Act).** Adopted in some form by approximately forty-six states. Provides a statutory framework allowing the personal representative or successor trustee to access digital assets, subject to the deceased's user-level directives at the platform. Most major platforms (Google, Apple, Facebook) now offer in-platform tools to designate post-death access. These tools are easy to set up during life and decisive at death.

2. **Cryptocurrency in self-custody.** If the deceased held cryptocurrency in a self-custody wallet — a hardware wallet, a paper wallet, a software wallet — and the family does not have the seed phrase or private keys, the assets are effectively unrecoverable. There is no court order that can reconstruct a lost private key. Self-custody requires explicit succession planning: the seed phrase recorded, secured, and accessible by the trusted successor. Without it, the assets

are lost.

3. **Subscriptions and recurring charges.** Cancel promptly. Identity theft against the deceased frequently begins with a compromised email account whose credentials were stored at a service the family did not know to cancel.

When the Will Cannot Be Found

If the original will cannot be located after death, the law presumes the deceased revoked it. This presumption can be rebutted, but the burden is on the proponent of a copy.

The path forward depends on what evidence is available:

- If a copy of the will exists, the proponent may petition to admit the copy with evidence rebutting the revocation presumption — for example, evidence that the original was lost in a flood, that the deceased's safe was emptied by a disinterested party, that the will was last in the attorney's office and the attorney's records confirm it.
- If no copy and no evidence exists, the estate is administered as intestate. The state's intestate-succession statute determines who takes.
- If a holographic (handwritten) instrument exists, the proponent may attempt to admit it as a valid will. State requirements for holographic wills vary considerably.

The most common reason a will cannot be found is poor storage. Recommended practice: keep the original with the drafting attorney's firm or in a fireproof home safe; keep a copy at the attorney's office; tell the named executor where the original is kept and how to access it. A will whose location is known is a will that gets admitted.

Insolvent Estates

An estate is insolvent when its valid debts and claims exceed its assets. Insolvent estates produce no distribution to beneficiaries; creditors are paid in priority order until assets are exhausted, and lower-priority creditors receive nothing.

Three practical points:

1. **Family is not personally liable.** Surviving family members are not personally responsible for the deceased's debts unless they co-signed or are otherwise on the obligation. Creditors who suggest otherwise are incorrect.

2. **The executor's role narrows.** In an insolvent estate, the executor's job becomes to marshal assets, evaluate claims, pay them in statutory priority order (Appendix M), and close the estate. There is nothing to distribute to beneficiaries.

3. **Some assets remain protected.** Life insurance with named beneficiaries, retirement accounts with named beneficiaries, jointly titled survivorship assets, and (in many

states) homestead property may pass outside the insolvency analysis. Creditors of the estate cannot reach these — though creditors of the beneficiary may.

> **KEY POINT**
>
> Special situations in probate are not exotic; they are common enough that a substantial minority of estates touch at least one of them. The estate plan that anticipates them — blended-family drafting, multi-state titling, special-needs trusts, digital-asset succession — handles them at a fraction of the cost a reactive estate would.

What This Looks Like in Practice

A man in his early seventies dies leaving a second wife of fourteen years, two adult children from a prior marriage, an adult son with a developmental disability who is on SSI, a vacation home in another state, and a small cryptocurrency position he managed himself.

If he had drafted with the special situations in mind, the result would have been clean. A QTIP trust would handle the blended-family interface — his wife with lifetime income, his children inheriting the principal at her death. A special-needs trust would receive his disabled son's share without disturbing benefits eligibility. A transfer-on-death deed in the second state would have moved the vacation home outside any ancillary proceeding. The cryptocurrency seed phrase would be in a sealed envelope with his attorney, indexed in his letter of instruction.

Without those preparations, his estate spends two years in probate. The blended-family interface produces a contested spousal-election proceeding. The disabled son's share, distributed outright through intestacy mechanics, costs him his SSI for two years before the family rebuilds the special-needs trust retroactively. The vacation home requires an ancillary proceeding the family did not anticipate. The cryptocurrency is permanently lost — the seed phrase was on a sticky note in a notebook that the family eventually discarded without recognizing it.

The two outcomes started from the same family, the same assets, the same affection between the deceased and his beneficiaries. They diverged on the basis of an afternoon of thoughtful drafting eight years before death — drafting that would have cost a few thousand dollars at the time and saved the family hundreds of thousands.

What This Chapter Has Said

Probate's textbook arc covers the majority of cases. Six categories of special situation produce most of the rest: blended families, multi-state real property, minor beneficiaries, beneficiaries with disabilities, digital assets, and missing-original-will cases. Each is anticipatable with appropriate drafting. None is so unusual that it should surprise an experienced practitioner. A small amount of attention paid in advance — typically less than the cost of one round of probate fees — handles all six categories cleanly.

The next section, the Conclusion, ties the threads of the book together.

READER FAQ

Common Questions, Clear Answers

◆

This section addresses, in brief Q-and-A form, the questions readers most commonly ask after finishing the book. The answers are intentionally short. Each one points back to the chapter or chapters where the underlying material is treated in full.

The questions are grouped into three categories. The first category — Estates & Trusts — covers probate proper and the trust-and-will interface that occupies the body of the book. The second category — Living Wills & Advance Directives — covers the lifetime instruments that often come up in the same conversation. The third category — Health & Medical Law — covers the small handful of medical-legal questions that arise during the last illness and the early estate.

ESTATES & TRUSTS

Q · DO I NEED PROBATE IF THERE IS A WILL?

A · Yes — the will is the document the probate court administers. Probate is the process; the will is the instructions. An estate with a will and individually titled assets goes through probate. Probate is avoided by instruments other than the will: trusts, joint titling, and beneficiary designations. See Chapters 1, 2, and 8.

Q · DO I NEED PROBATE IF THERE IS NO WILL?

A · Almost certainly yes, if the deceased held individually titled assets at death. Without a will, the court applies the state's intestate-succession statute to determine who takes. The procedure is otherwise similar. See Chapter 2 and Chapter 8.

Q · HOW LONG DOES PROBATE TAKE?

A · Eight to twelve months for an uncontested estate of ordinary complexity. Six to seven months is unusually fast. Twelve to twenty-four months is common when business interests, multi-state real property, or estate-tax filings are involved. Three to five years is realistic when the estate is contested. See Chapter 6 and Table 6.2.

Q · HOW MUCH DOES PROBATE COST?

A · Most ordinary estates spend three to seven percent of the gross estate on probate-related fees and costs. The figure varies by state, by complexity, and by whether litigation is required. The widely repeated claim that probate costs half the estate is essentially never true in the ordinary case. See Chapter 8 and Table 8.1.

Q · DO I NEED A LAWYER TO PROBATE AN ESTATE?

A · In most states the personal representative is permitted but not required to engage counsel for ordinary uncontested administration. As a practical matter, all but the smallest estates benefit substantially from probate counsel — fees are paid from the estate, not personally, and the cost is almost always less than the cost of mistakes the executor would otherwise make. See Chapter 4.

Q · CAN I AVOID PROBATE ENTIRELY?

A · Often yes — by titling assets in a properly funded revocable trust, by using payable-on-death and transfer-on-death designations, and by joint titling with right of survivorship. Whether to do so depends on family circumstances and on the trade-offs probate offers (creditor cutoff, court oversight). See Chapters 2 and 8 and the companion volume Trust Made Simple.

Q · WHAT IS LETTERS TESTAMENTARY?

A · The court-issued document that confirms the executor's appointment and authority to act for the estate. Banks, brokerages, and county recorders require it before they will speak with the executor. See Chapter 3.

Q · MUST I ACCEPT THE ROLE OF EXECUTOR?

A · No. Decline is permitted. The will typically names a successor; if not, the court appoints one based on statutory priority. Decline is not a failure; it is sometimes the most responsible option. See Chapter 4.

Q · WHAT IF I CAN'T FIND THE ORIGINAL WILL?

A · The estate may be administered as intestate, or the proponent may attempt to admit a copy with evidence rebutting the presumption of revocation. Both paths are slower and costlier than admission of the original. See Chapter 7.

Q · ARE PROBATE FILINGS PUBLIC?

A · Yes, with very few exceptions. The will, the inventory, the accounting, and the orders are public records in most states. This is one of the principal reasons families use trusts when privacy is a priority. See Chapter 8.

Q · CAN A BENEFICIARY DEMAND AN ACCOUNTING?

A · Yes, in nearly every state. Beneficiaries are entitled to a formal accounting before final distribution, and many jurisdictions allow interim accountings on request. See Chapter 4 and Chapter 7.

Q · WHAT HAPPENS TO DEBTS THE DECEASED OWED?

A · Valid debts of the deceased are paid by the estate, in a statutory priority order, before any distribution to beneficiaries. If the estate is insolvent, debts are paid in priority and lower-priority creditors may receive nothing. Surviving family members are not personally liable for the deceased's debts unless they co-signed or are otherwise on the obligation. See Chapter 4 and Chapter 6.

Q · DO RETIREMENT ACCOUNTS GO THROUGH PROBATE?

A · Not if a living beneficiary is designated. The named beneficiary takes outside probate by contract with the custodian. If no beneficiary is named (or all named beneficiaries have died), the account typically defaults to the estate and becomes a probate asset. See Chapter 2.

Q · DOES LIFE INSURANCE GO THROUGH PROBATE?

A · Not if a living beneficiary is designated. Insurance proceeds are paid directly to the beneficiary outside probate. If no beneficiary is named, or the policy is payable to the estate, the proceeds are a probate asset. See Chapter 2.

Q · WHAT IS ANCILLARY PROBATE?

A · A separate probate proceeding in a state where the deceased owned real property, when that state is different from the deceased's state of residence. The principal probate runs in the home state; an ancillary proceeding handles the out-of-state real property. See Chapter 7.

Q · CAN A WILL BE CONTESTED AFTER ADMISSION TO PROBATE?

A · Yes, within a statutory window — typically a few months from notice of admission. Grounds include lack of capacity, undue influence, fraud, and improper execution. Contests are evidentiary, expensive, and statistically unlikely to succeed. See Chapter 7 and Table 7.1.

Q · WHAT IS A NO-CONTEST CLAUSE?

A · A provision in the will that disinherits a beneficiary who challenges the will and loses. State enforcement varies — some states do not enforce the clauses at all; most enforce them unless the contestant had probable cause. See Chapter 7.

Q · WHAT HAPPENS IF THE EXECUTOR DOES NOT DO THE JOB?

A · Beneficiaries may petition the court for an interim accounting, for instructions, or — in serious cases — for the executor's removal. After closing, beneficiaries may sue an executor personally for any loss attributable to fiduciary breach. See Chapter 7.

Q · WHAT IS A POUR-OVER WILL?

A · A short will whose only function is to direct any asset that was not transferred into the deceased's revocable trust during life into the trust at death. It is the safety net for trust-based estate plans. See Chapter 2.

Q · DOES PROBATE END FOREVER?

A · Yes. Once the court closes the estate and discharges the executor, the estate as a legal entity ceases to exist. Most categories of subsequent claim are barred. Some narrow categories — fraud, willful misconduct, previously unknown creditors — can survive in limited circumstances. See Chapter 10.

Q · I HAVE BOTH A WILL AND A REVOCABLE TRUST. WHICH CONTROLS?

A · Both, but for different assets. The trust controls whatever is titled in the trust's name. The will (typically a pour-over will in this setup) controls anything left in your individual name at death — and directs those assets back into the trust at the close of probate. The pour-over will must still be admitted to probate, even when the trust holds most of the estate. See Chapter 11.

Q · WHAT IS THE "FUNDING GAP" IN A TRUST PLAN?

A · Any asset that the settlor of a revocable trust intended to place in the trust but failed to retitle during life. At death, the unfunded asset is a probate residue — the pour-over will catches it, but it must pass through probate first. The funding gap is the most common single failure in modern estate planning. An annual review of titles and beneficiary designations prevents nearly all of it. See Chapter 11.

Q · I HAVE A FAMILY MEMBER ON SSI/MEDICAID. HOW DO I LEAVE THEM SOMETHING?

A · Through a special-needs trust (SNT), drafted in advance and ready to receive their share at death. The SNT supplements rather than replaces the beneficiary's public benefits and is not a countable resource for eligibility. Outright distribution to a beneficiary on means-tested benefits typically disqualifies them. Pooled trusts are an option for smaller distributions; disclaimers are an option for retroactive planning. See Chapter 12.

Q · WHAT HAPPENS TO MY CRYPTOCURRENCY WHEN I DIE?

A · If it is held in a self-custody wallet — a hardware wallet, paper wallet, or software wallet — and your family does not have the seed phrase or private keys, the assets are unrecoverable. There is no court order that can reconstruct a lost private key. Self-custody requires explicit succession planning: record the seed phrase, secure it, and make it accessible to the trusted successor. Cryptocurrency held at a regulated exchange follows the exchange's beneficiary or estate-claim procedure. See Chapter 12.

Q · I OWN A VACATION HOME IN ANOTHER STATE. WILL THAT TRIGGER A SECOND PROBATE?

A · Yes — an ancillary probate in the second state — unless the property is held in a way that bypasses probate. Three options: (1) title the property in a revocable trust during life, (2) record a transfer-on-death deed if the second state recognizes them, or (3) hold the property through a single-member LLC owned by the trust. Each avoids the ancillary proceeding entirely. See Chapter 12 and Appendix N.

Q · MY PARENT'S WILL CANNOT BE FOUND. WHAT NOW?

A · The law presumes the will was revoked unless the proponent of a copy can rebut the presumption with evidence (e.g., the original was lost in a flood, the deceased's safe was emptied by a disinterested party). If a copy and supporting evidence exist, the copy may be admitted to probate. If neither exists, the estate is administered as intestate under state law. Holographic wills (handwritten, signed by the testator) are recognized in some states with reduced formality. See Chapter 12.

Q · CAN MY FAMILY BE HELD PERSONALLY LIABLE FOR MY DEBTS WHEN I DIE?

A · No, unless they co-signed or are otherwise on the obligation. Surviving family members are not personally responsible for the deceased's debts. Debts are paid from the estate's assets in statutory priority order; if the estate is insolvent, lower-priority creditors receive nothing. Creditors who suggest otherwise are incorrect. See Chapter 12 and Appendix M.

LIVING WILLS & ADVANCE DIRECTIVES

Q · WHAT IS A LIVING WILL, AND HOW IS IT DIFFERENT FROM A WILL?

A · A living will is an instruction to medical providers about the kind of treatment a person wants — or does not want — if they cannot make their own decisions. It operates during life, in a medical setting. A will, by contrast, operates only after death and addresses the distribution of property. The two instruments share a name but solve different problems. A complete estate plan typically includes both. The living will has no role in probate; it has no effect on title to property; it ends the moment the person dies.

Q · WHAT IS AN ADVANCE DIRECTIVE OR HEALTHCARE PROXY, AND HOW DOES IT INTERACT WITH PROBATE?

A · An advance directive (sometimes called a healthcare proxy or durable power of attorney for healthcare) names an agent authorized to make medical decisions when the principal cannot. It does not interact with probate at all — its authority ends at death. The probate court takes over from there. A well-prepared family has both: an advance directive for the last illness, and an estate plan for what comes after.

Q · MY PARENT NEVER SIGNED A LIVING WILL OR ADVANCE DIRECTIVE. WHAT NOW?

A · If your parent is still alive but cannot make decisions, the family may need to seek a court-appointed guardian or conservator. The procedure varies by state but is its own proceeding, separate from probate. If your parent has died, the absence of an advance directive does not affect probate — probate is about property, not about the medical decisions that preceded death. Going forward, every adult should complete an advance-directive form for their state; most states make the form available at no cost online.

Q · DOES A LIVING WILL OR ADVANCE DIRECTIVE NEED TO BE FILED WITH THE COURT?

A · No. Both are private documents. Provide signed copies to your primary physician, your hospital of choice, your healthcare-proxy agent, and your estate-planning attorney. Keep one copy at home in a known location. Some states maintain a voluntary registry; participation is optional and does not change the document's legal effect.

HEALTH & MEDICAL LAW

Q · ARE UNPAID MEDICAL BILLS CLAIMS AGAINST THE ESTATE?

A · Yes. Medical providers are creditors of the estate and present claims in the same way other creditors do. Last-illness expenses receive a high priority in most states' statutory payment order — typically behind administration costs and funeral expenses but ahead of ordinary unsecured debts. See Appendix M for the full priority order.

Q · AS EXECUTOR, CAN I ACCESS MY PARENT'S MEDICAL RECORDS UNDER HIPAA?

A · After death, the executor (or personal representative) generally has the legal authority of the deceased for purposes of HIPAA — meaning the executor may request medical records, including for the period before death, on presentation of Letters Testamentary. Providers vary in how they handle the request; expect to provide a death certificate, the Letters, and a written request. See Chapter 4.

Q · WHAT HAPPENS TO MEDICARE, MEDICAID, AND PRIVATE HEALTH INSURANCE AT DEATH?

A · Medicare and Medicaid coverage end at death; pending claims are evaluated and paid through the date of death. Medicaid programs in many states have estate-recovery provisions — meaning the state may file a creditor claim for benefits paid during a recipient's life. The recovery is limited by federal rules and varies by state; in estates with a surviving spouse or minor children, recovery is often deferred or waived. Private health insurance ends at death; pending claims are paid; cancel coverage promptly to avoid posthumous premium charges.

Q · ARE FUNERAL AND BURIAL EXPENSES PAID BEFORE OTHER DEBTS?

A · Yes, in nearly every state. Funeral and burial expenses receive a high statutory priority — typically second only to administration costs (court fees, executor compensation, attorney fees). They are paid before ordinary creditors. See Appendix M, Table M.1. Practical consequence: a family member who advances funds for funeral expenses is entitled to reimbursement from the estate, ahead of most other creditors.

Q · DOES A LIVING WILL AFFECT WHETHER PROBATE HAPPENS?

A · No. The living will controls medical decisions during life. Probate is triggered by the existence of probate property at death — that is, by titling, not by medical decisions. The two instruments operate in different worlds. The presence or absence of a living will neither triggers nor prevents probate.

GLOSSARY OF PROBATE TERMS

◆

This glossary covers the principal terms used in this book, in alphabetical order. Each entry includes a brief definition and, where helpful, a cross-reference to the chapter where the term is treated in fuller context.

Abatement
The reduction of legacies when the estate is insufficient to satisfy all bequests. Statutory order generally is: residuary, then general, then specific. See Chapter 4.

Accounting
The formal record of an estate's receipts, disbursements, and proposed distributions, prepared by the personal representative for review by the beneficiaries and the court before closing. See Chapters 4 and 10.

Administrator
The court-appointed person who administers an estate when there is no will or no will-named executor able to serve. See Chapter 4.

Ancillary Probate
A separate probate proceeding in a state where the deceased owned real property, conducted in addition to the principal probate in the state of residence. See Chapter 7.

Beneficiary
A person or entity entitled to receive property from an estate or trust. See Chapter 2.

Bond (Fiduciary)
A surety instrument that protects beneficiaries against loss caused by the executor's misconduct. Required in many states unless waived by the will. See Chapter 4.

Codicil

A formal amendment to a will, executed with the same statutory formalities required of the original will. See Chapter 7.

Conservatorship / Guardianship of the Estate

Court-supervised management of an incapacitated person's property during life — distinct from probate, though sometimes appearing in the same court. See Chapter 5.

Creditor's Claim

A formal demand for payment, presented to the personal representative during the statutory claim window. Claims not presented in the window are time-barred. See Chapter 6 and Table 6.1.

Decedent

The person who has died. The standard legal term used throughout probate practice.

Devise

A gift of real property under a will. (Personal property under a will is a "bequest.") Modern usage often blurs the distinction.

Executor

The person named in a will to administer the estate, confirmed by the court through issuance of Letters Testamentary. See Chapter 4.

Fiduciary

A person who holds legal authority to act on behalf of another, with a duty of loyalty, care, and accountability enforceable in court. The executor is a fiduciary. See Chapter 4.

Heir

A person entitled by intestate succession to a share of an estate. Heirs are determined by state statute when there is no will. See Chapter 2.

Holographic Will

A handwritten will, signed by the testator, recognized in some states with reduced execution formalities. See Chapter 7.

Inheritance
Property received from a deceased person, whether by will, trust, intestate succession, or non-probate transfer.

Intestate / Intestate Succession
Dying without a valid will. The state's intestate-succession statute determines distribution. See Chapter 2 and Chapter 8.

Inventory
The formal list of probate assets and their date-of-death values, filed with the court within the statutory window after appointment. See Chapter 4.

Letters Testamentary / Letters of Administration
The court-issued documents that confirm an executor's or administrator's authority. Letters Testamentary issue when there is a will; Letters of Administration when there is not. See Chapter 3.

Lodging the Will
The administrative filing of the original will with the probate court shortly after death, typically required by statute. See Chapter 3.

No-Contest Clause (In Terrorem)
A will provision disinheriting a beneficiary who challenges the will and loses. Enforcement varies by state. See Chapter 7.

Notice to Creditors
The published and direct notice given by the personal representative informing creditors that an estate is open and that claims must be presented within the statutory window. See Chapter 6.

Per Stirpes / Per Capita
Two methods of dividing an estate among descendants. Per stirpes passes a deceased beneficiary's share to that beneficiary's descendants; per capita divides equally among living individuals at the named generation. See Chapter 4.

Personal Representative
The modern unified term covering both executors (under a will) and administrators (intestate). See Chapter 4.

POD / TOD

Payable-on-death (POD) and transfer-on-death (TOD) designations on bank and brokerage accounts that pass the asset directly to the designated beneficiary outside probate. See Chapter 2.

Pour-Over Will

A short will whose only purpose is to direct any asset not previously placed in a trust into that trust at death. Used as a backstop for trust-based estate plans. See Chapter 2 and Chapter 11.

QTIP Trust

Qualified Terminable Interest Property trust. A marital trust that provides lifetime income to a surviving spouse while preserving the remainder for beneficiaries the deceased spouse named — typically used in blended-family planning. See Chapter 12.

RUFADAA

Revised Uniform Fiduciary Access to Digital Assets Act. The statutory framework — adopted in some form by most U.S. states — that permits a personal representative or successor trustee to access the deceased's digital accounts. See Chapter 12.

Special-Needs Trust (SNT)

A trust designed to hold a distribution for a beneficiary receiving means-tested public benefits (SSI, Medicaid) without disqualifying the beneficiary from those benefits. The trust supplements rather than replaces public assistance. See Chapter 12.

Funding Gap

An asset that the settlor of a revocable trust intended to place in the trust but failed to retitle during life. The asset becomes a probate residue at death and is poured over to the trust by the pour-over will. See Chapter 11.

UTMA / UGMA

Uniform Transfers to Minors Act / Uniform Gifts to Minors Act. State statutes that allow a custodian to hold property for a minor until the minor reaches majority. See Chapter 12.

Transfer-on-Death Deed (TOD Deed / Lady-Bird Deed)

A recorded deed that transfers real property automatically at death without any probate proceeding, recognized by approximately half of U.S. states. See Chapter 2 and Chapter 12.

Probate Estate

The set of assets that pass through probate at death. Distinguished from the gross estate (which includes non-probate assets for tax purposes). See Chapter 2.

Residuary Estate

What remains of the estate after specific bequests, debts, taxes, and expenses have been paid. The residuary clause of a will controls. See Chapter 4.

Self-Proving Affidavit

An affidavit attached to a will, signed by the testator and witnesses, attesting to proper execution. Allows the will to be admitted to probate without live testimony from the witnesses. See Chapter 7.

Small-Estate Affidavit

A statutory procedure allowing the transfer of small estates without full probate. The dollar threshold and procedure vary by state. See Chapter 2 and Table 2.2.

Spousal Election / Forced Share

Statutory protection for a surviving spouse against being entirely disinherited by will. The spouse may elect to take a statutory share rather than the will's bequest. See Chapter 7.

Successor Trustee

The trustee who takes over administration of a trust upon the death or incapacity of the original trustee. See companion volume, Trust Made Simple.

Surcharge Action

A lawsuit by a beneficiary against an executor or trustee, seeking recovery for losses attributable to fiduciary breach. See Chapter 7.

Testator / Testatrix

The person who has executed a will. The female-form variant testatrix is largely retired in modern practice.

Undue Influence

Wrongful pressure exerted on a testator to substitute the influencer's intent for the testator's own. A common ground for will contest, with high evidentiary burdens. See Chapter 7 and Table 7.1.

Uniform Probate Code (UPC)

A model statute, adopted in some form by approximately one-third of states, that aims to standardize probate practice. States vary in how fully they have adopted it. See Chapter 1.

Will Contest

A formal challenge to the validity of a will, brought in the probate court within a statutory window. See Chapter 7.

BIBLIOGRAPHY & REFERENCE GUIDE

◆

This bibliography lists the principal sources consulted in preparing this volume, organized by category. It is not exhaustive. It is intended as a reading map for the serious reader who wishes to investigate the underlying material in greater depth.

STATUTORY AND REGULATORY SOURCES

Uniform Probate Code (UPC), National Conference of Commissioners on Uniform State Laws, as adopted (in modified form) in approximately one-third of U.S. states. Available at the Uniform Law Commission website.

California Probate Code, Divisions 7 (Administration of Estates of Decedents) and 11 (Construction of Wills, Trusts, and Other Instruments).

Florida Statutes, Title XLII (Estates and Trusts), Chapters 731–735 (probate, summary administration, and disposition without administration).

Texas Estates Code, Titles 1 (General Provisions) and 2 (Estates of Decedents; Durable Powers of Attorney), as recodified from the former Texas Probate Code.

New York Surrogate's Court Procedure Act (SCPA) and Estates, Powers and Trusts Law (EPTL).

Pennsylvania Consolidated Statutes, Title 20 (Decedents, Estates and Fiduciaries Code).

Illinois Compiled Statutes, Chapter 755 (Estates), particularly the Probate Act of 1975 (755 ILCS 5).

Internal Revenue Code, Subtitle B (Estate and Gift Taxes) and Subchapter J (Estates, Trusts, Beneficiaries, and Decedents).

TREATISES

Bogert, Bogert & Hess, The Law of Trusts and Trustees (3d ed., Thomson Reuters). The standard American treatise on trust law, with extensive treatment of the trust-versus-probate interface.

Atkinson, Handbook of the Law of Wills (2d ed., West). Classic treatment of will law and probate procedure, retained in many academic libraries.

Page, Page on the Law of Wills (Anderson). Multi-volume treatise; the most exhaustive American treatment of testamentary instruments.

Restatement (Third) of Property: Wills and Other Donative Transfers, American Law Institute. The current synthesis of American law on wills, intestate succession, and gratuitous transfers.

Restatement (Third) of Trusts, American Law Institute. The current synthesis of American trust law, with cross-references to probate matters.

Pennell, Federal Wealth Transfer Taxation (West). Standard advanced text on federal estate, gift, and generation-skipping transfer taxes.

Bittker & Lokken, Federal Taxation of Income, Estates and Gifts (Thomson Reuters). Multi-volume treatise.

PRACTITIONER GUIDES

American College of Trust and Estate Counsel (ACTEC) Commentaries on the Model Rules of Professional Conduct (most recent edition). Practitioner guidance on the ethics of probate representation.

Beyer, Wills, Trusts, and Estates: Examples & Explanations (Wolters Kluwer). Plain-language overview useful for non-specialists.

Sitkoff & Dukeminier, Wills, Trusts, and Estates (Aspen Casebook Series, Wolters Kluwer). The leading academic casebook in the field; useful for context.

American Bar Association, Guide to Wills and Estates (current edition). Practical introduction for non-lawyers.

HISTORICAL SOURCES

Maitland, Equity, ed. Brunyate. The classic study of the equity courts and the development of trust and probate doctrine. Originally published 1909.

Pollock & Maitland, The History of English Law Before the Time of Edward I (2d ed., 1898; reissued by Cambridge University Press). Foundational treatment of the early English probate jurisdiction.

Helmholz, The Oxford History of the Laws of England, Vol. I (Ecclesiastical Jurisdiction). The pre-Reformation ecclesiastical courts that originated probate jurisdiction in England.

FAMILY-WEALTH AND LEGACY LITERATURE

Hughes, Family Wealth: Keeping It in the Family. The seminal work on multi-generational family wealth dynamics.

Collier, Wealth in Families. Harvard study of inherited-wealth dynamics across generations.

Daniell, Family Legacy and Leadership. Practitioner treatment of family governance and the human dimensions of legacy.

PERIODICALS

Estate Planning journal (Thomson Reuters), monthly. Practitioner-oriented; widely read.

Trusts & Estates magazine, monthly. Long-running industry publication.

Probate & Property magazine, ABA Real Property, Trust and Estate Law Section. Bimonthly practitioner publication.

ACTEC Law Journal (American College of Trust and Estate Counsel), three times annually. Scholarly.

ONLINE AND PRACTITIONER RESOURCES

ACTEC website and Fellows directory (actec.org). The leading professional society for trust and estate practitioners.

American Bar Association, Section of Real Property, Trust and Estate Law (americanbar.org/groups/real_property_trust_estate).

National Association of Estate Planners & Councils (NAEPC; naepc.org). Multi-disciplinary professional organization.

Steve Leimberg's LISI (Leimberg Information Services). Practitioner email-based service with frequent commentary on estate-administration developments.

Court self-help offices. Most state probate courts maintain a self-help division for unrepresented litigants. The materials are useful for non-lawyers seeking the procedural mechanics in their own jurisdiction.

ABOUT THE PUBLISHER

AVOY, LLC ("AVOY Publishing") is the publishing imprint of AVOY, LLC, a privately held company headquartered in the United States. AVOY Publishing exists to bring institutional-grade reference material on private wealth, legacy planning, family governance, and the procedural realities of American private law to readers who would otherwise rely on marketing brochures and law-review articles.

The Complete Estate & Property Planning Series is the imprint's flagship project — a four-book institutional reference that, taken together, addresses the four pillars of American post-mortem asset transfer: the trust as instrument, the probate process, the disposition of real property, and the transfer-tax regime. Each volume in the series is built to the same standard: a sophisticated subject treated with care, written for the intelligent reader rather than the specialist, structured for both first reading and long-term reference, and produced to a physical and editorial quality that respects the seriousness of the subject.

The four books in The Complete Estate & Property Planning Series:

- Book 1 — Trust Made Simple

- Book 2 — Probate Explained (this volume)
- Book 3 — Property After Death
- Book 4 — Estate Taxes Explained

Probate Explained is Book 2 of the series, picking up where Trust Made Simple leaves off and treating the probate process itself in the same plain-language style. Book 3 (Property After Death) drills into real-property disposition; Book 4 (Estate Taxes Explained) completes the series by treating the federal and state transfer-tax regime.

AVOY Publishing books are distributed in print (paperback and hardcover), Kindle eBook, and audiobook formats through Amazon and other retailers.

Inquiries: ap@avoyhq.com

ABOUT THE AUTHOR

◆

A. Perkins writes for people who would rather understand a thing than be told what to think about it.

A #1 Amazon bestselling author, former United States Air Force nuclear missile launch officer, holder of an MBA, and a working chief executive, he has spent his career at the intersection of high-stakes systems and ordinary human consequence. Born in Mississippi and raised in East St. Louis, Illinois, he is among the rare voices in legacy-planning literature to have navigated generational poverty, institutional pressure, and significant personal and financial trials — and to have emerged with a single, durable conviction: that everyday Americans, properly informed and properly equipped, can build extraordinary protection for the people they love.

His prior body of work — including the bestselling 21 Bars: Poetry from the Inside and Urban Poetry & Truth: The Echo of the Streets; Whispers to Mom: A Collection of Poems Celebrating Love, Resilience, and Mothers; The Intimacy Life Cycle: Fire – Fizzle – Fire; Stillness Starts Here; Beyond the Vail: An Awakening; Whispers of Love and Life — Part II; and the institutional-grade reference volume Trust Made Simple — spans poetry, mindfulness, and the lived terrain of resilience, alongside the legacy-planning subjects he has been studying for more than a decade. Across more than twenty prior volumes — each released in both print and audiobook — and three Amazon bestseller categories, he has built a readership that returns to him for one reason above all: the willingness to tell the truth in plain language.

Probate Explained is his twenty-second book in print, the second dedicated to the field of legacy planning, and Book 2 of The Complete Estate & Property Planning Series — following Trust Made Simple (Book 1) and preceding Property After Death (Book 3) and Estate Taxes Explained (Book 4). It grows out of more than a decade of practical, personal experience with the administration of estates and trusts, years of close study of the probate codes of multiple states, and the conviction that probate — properly understood — is one of the most reliable institutions in American private law for the family that arrives at it informed. Like every prior title in his catalog, it is also available in an audiobook edition.

Mr. Perkins is the founder and chief executive of AVOY, LLC, parent of AVOY Publishing and The Complete Estate & Property Planning Series. He continues to write, teach, and speak on protection, legacy, and the long arithmetic of family wealth.

For editorial and speaking inquiries: ap@avoyhq.com

PART

APPENDICES

Reference material — checklists, samples, and supplementary tools.

APPENDIX A

Probate at a Glance

This appendix is a single-card reference summarizing the entire probate process in one place. It is intended to be torn from the book and kept with the executor's working file, or reproduced electronically and shared among co-executors and family members.

Table A.1

Phase	Typical timing	Principal task
Death and immediate aftermath	Days 1–7	Death certificate, secure residence, locate will.
Estate-opening preparation	Weeks 2–4	Engage counsel, lodge will, prepare petition.
Petition for probate filed	Week 4–8	Notice given; first hearing scheduled.
Letters issued	Week 6–10	Personal representative formally appointed.
Inventory and appraisal	Months 2–4	Identify and value all probate assets.
Notice to creditors published	Month 2–3	Creditor-claim window opens (3–7 months in most states).
Tax returns filed	Months 3–9	Decedent's final 1040; estate's 1041; Form 706 if required.
Creditor claims evaluated and paid	Months 4–9	Valid claims paid; rejected claims contested if pursued.
Petition for distribution	Months 9–12	Final accounting prepared; distribution proposed.
Court approval of accounting	Months 11–14	Hearing on accounting; objections resolved.
Distribution and closing	Months 12–18	Assets transferred; receipts collected; estate closed.

The probate process at a glance.

Timing varies by state, by estate complexity, and by whether disputes arise. Use Table 6.2 in Chapter 6 for a more nuanced timeline by estate type.

APPENDIX B

Small-Estate Procedures by State

Tables 2.2 and 6.1 in Parts I and III provide the principal state-by-state comparisons for small-estate thresholds and creditor-claim windows. Readers preparing for a probate-court appointment may find it useful to review those tables together with the additional summary below.

Three patterns in the small-estate landscape are worth noting:

1. **Thresholds rise.** Most state legislatures revise small-estate thresholds upward every four to six years. The current figure for any state is a phone call to the probate clerk away — and that call should be made before assuming a small-estate procedure does or does not apply.
2. **Real property complicates everything.** Most small-estate procedures apply to personal property only. Estates with even a single parcel of real property usually require either a full probate or a separate court-supervised set-aside proceeding. A few states (notably California) provide a Spousal Property Petition that can transfer real property to a surviving spouse without full probate.
3. **Speed varies sharply.** A small-estate affidavit can be executed and used to collect assets in two to four weeks in

many states. A summary-administration proceeding (Florida) can close in eight to twelve weeks. A formal probate of an estate that just exceeded the threshold can take eight to twelve months. The size of the savings produced by careful planning around the threshold is sometimes substantial.

The single best source of current state-specific information is the self-help division of the probate court in the relevant county. Self-help offices typically maintain free packets describing the procedure, the threshold, the required forms, and the filing fee.

APPENDIX C

The Executor's First-Sixty-Days Checklist

The first sixty days of an executor's role include the heaviest concentration of administrative activity in the entire estate administration. This checklist covers the principal items and is organized roughly chronologically.

Days 1–7

- Order ten to fifteen original death certificates from the funeral home or vital-records office.
- Locate the original will, any codicils, any trust agreement, durable powers of attorney, advance directives, and the deceased's letter of instruction (if any).
- Secure the deceased's residence — locks, mail, perishables, pets, vehicles.
- Notify immediate family members and close associates of the death.
- Identify the deceased's primary financial relationships: bank, brokerage, retirement custodian, life insurance, employer (if any), payroll.

 Begin assembling a single binder or digital folder of estate documents.

 Forward mail to the executor's address (USPS forwarding form).

 Place a credit freeze with the three credit bureaus to prevent identity theft.

Days 8–21

 Engage probate counsel for a no-cost or low-cost initial meeting.

 Lodge the original will with the probate court (administrative filing — does not yet open the proceeding).

 Notify financial institutions of the death and provide each with a death certificate.

 Cancel credit cards in the deceased's individual name.

 Cancel subscriptions, club memberships, gym memberships, and other recurring auto-pays.

 Cancel the deceased's driver's license with the state DMV.

 Identify and inventory safe-deposit boxes (you may need a court order to open one before letters issue).

 Begin a preliminary list of debts — credit cards, mortgages, medical bills, utilities — without yet acting on them.

Days 22–45

 Prepare and file the petition for probate with the appropriate court.

 Give notice to heirs and beneficiaries of the petition and hearing date.

 Apply for the estate's Employer Identification Number (EIN) from the IRS (Form SS-4).

 Begin compiling a preliminary inventory: real property, accounts, retirement, life insurance, business interests, vehicles, household goods.

 Begin obtaining date-of-death valuations for major assets (real estate appraisal, brokerage statement, retirement-account statement).

 Discuss the question of executor compensation, surety bond, and waiver-of-bond with counsel.

Days 46–60

 Attend the first hearing on the petition; receive the court's order admitting the will and appointing the executor.

 Receive Letters Testamentary (or Letters of Administration) from the court clerk; obtain at least five certified copies.

 Open the estate bank account using the Letters and the EIN.

- Transfer the deceased's individual-account balances into the estate account.
- Publish the notice to creditors as directed by counsel.
- Send direct notice to known creditors.
- File the deceased's final personal-income-tax return for the prior year if not yet filed.
- Engage a CPA or tax preparer for the estate's annual tax return (Form 1041) and, if required, the federal estate-tax return (Form 706).
- Schedule a meeting with the beneficiaries to communicate the calendar and expectations for the next several months.

By the end of the first sixty days, an executor who has worked through this checklist is well-positioned for the remainder of the administration. Almost every estate that closes on time does so because the first sixty days were handled with discipline.

APPENDIX D

Common Probate Forms and What They Mean

Probate generates a great deal of paper. This appendix names the forms that recur most often, in plain language, so executors and beneficiaries can recognize what they are looking at when a document arrives in the mail.

Table D.1

Document	Purpose	Who prepares
Petition for Probate	Asks the court to admit the will and appoint the executor.	Executor's counsel.
Notice of Petition to Administer Estate	Notifies heirs and beneficiaries of the hearing.	Executor's counsel.
Order for Probate	Court's order admitting the will and appointing the executor.	Court.
Letters Testamentary / Letters of Administration	Confirms the executor's authority for use with banks, brokerages, recorders.	Court clerk.
Inventory and Appraisal	Lists all probate assets at date-of-death value.	Executor (with appraiser support).
Notice to Creditors	Published notice opening the creditor-claim window.	Executor's counsel; published in newspaper.
Creditor's Claim	Formal demand for payment by a creditor.	Creditor.
Allowance or Rejection of Claim	Executor's response to a creditor's claim.	Executor.
Petition for Final Distribution	Asks the court to approve the accounting and authorize distribution.	Executor's counsel.
Final Accounting	Detailed record of all receipts, disbursements, and proposed distributions.	Executor (with accountant or counsel).
Order for Final Distribution	Court's order authorizing distribution.	Court.
Receipts on Distribution	Beneficiary's signed acknowledgment of distribution received.	Beneficiary; collected by executor.
Order Discharging Executor	Closes the estate and releases the executor.	Court.

Common probate documents and their function.

Each of these documents has a specific function in the procedure. Recognizing them on receipt is most of the work of being able to track an estate through its course.

APPENDIX E

Sample Letter of Instruction

A letter of instruction is a non-binding, informal document, written by the deceased during life, that tells the eventual executor and the family where things are, who to call, and how to begin. It is not a will, and it does not modify a will. It is the orientation document the family wishes existed at the moment of greatest confusion.

The following is a sample, adapted from common practitioner conventions. Real letters of instruction should be drafted to the family's specific circumstances and updated annually.

SAMPLE

To my family and to the executor of my estate — This letter is not part of my will and does not modify it. It is offered to help you find what you will need, in the order you will need it, in the days and weeks after my death. Updated [date]. (1) Original documents. My original will, trust agreement, and durable powers of attorney are kept in [location]. A duplicate copy of the will is held by [attorney name and firm]. (2) Important advisors. My estate-planning attorney is [name, firm, phone]. My CPA is [name, firm, phone]. My financial advisor is [name, firm, phone]. My life-insurance agent is [name, firm, phone]. (3) Banks and brokerages. My principal bank account is [bank name, account type — check stub or statement attached]. My brokerage account is [firm, account number on statement]. My retirement accounts are [list]. (4) Real property. I own real property at [list addresses, with deed location]. (5) Insurance. I have life insurance with [carrier, policy number]. I have property and casualty insurance with [carrier]. (6) Business interests. I hold an interest in [entity, percentage]. Operating documents are in [location]. (7) Digital. My password manager is [name]; the master password is held by [trusted person] and the backup is in [location]. (8) Funeral wishes. My preferences are [burial / cremation], [location], [other]. (9) Personal property memorandum. A separate signed memorandum, referenced in the will, lists my preferred distribution of items of tangible personal property. It is in [location]. (10) People to call. The first calls should be to [trusted person 1] and [trusted person 2]. They know to expect this and will help orient the family. (11) Things I would like you to know. [Personal notes — values, hopes, gratitudes, an explanation for any unequal distribution if applicable]. With love and gratitude, [Signature] [Date]

A letter of instruction is one of the highest-value, lowest-cost documents in the entire field of estate planning. It costs nothing to produce and saves the family weeks of confusion when the time comes.

APPENDIX F

Annotated Reading List for the Serious Reader

Readers who finish this volume and want to continue should consider the following sources. They are not arranged in order of importance; each addresses a different aspect of probate, estate administration, or the broader landscape of legacy planning.

Sitkoff & Dukeminier, Wills, Trusts, and Estates. The leading academic casebook in the field. Verbose by intent; useful for the reader who wants the law in extended discussion.

Beyer, Wills, Trusts, and Estates: Examples & Explanations. A plain-language survey, useful as a reading companion or reference for the non-lawyer working alongside counsel.

American Bar Association, Guide to Wills and Estates. Compact introduction written for a general audience.

Sharp & Dembiec, How to Probate an Estate (state-specific titles, Nolo Press). Practical guides written for the executor without counsel; quality varies by jurisdiction.

Hughes, Family Wealth: Keeping It in the Family. Not a probate book but the most influential single volume on multi-generational wealth dynamics, which is the field probate is one entry into.

Trust Made Simple (AVOY Publishing, 2026). The companion volume to this book, treating trusts in the same plain-language style. Reading the two together gives the reader a complete picture of how property moves at and after death.

ACTEC Foundation educational materials (actecfoundation.org). Free consumer-oriented summaries of estate-planning concepts.

AARP, Estate Planning Resources (aarp.org/money/estate-planning). Free overview material aimed at the general public; useful for orientation.

APPENDIX G

The Twelve-Month Estate Administration Calendar

This calendar is a month-by-month overview of what a typical, uncontested probate case looks like for the executor working with counsel and a CPA. Actual cases vary; some milestones occur earlier or later. Use the calendar as orientation, not as a deadline schedule.

Table G.1

Month	Principal activities	Court touch points
1	Death certificates, locate will, secure residence, engage counsel.	Lodge will (administrative).
2	Petition prepared, EIN obtained, preliminary inventory, notice to heirs.	Petition filed; first hearing scheduled.
3	First hearing held; Letters issued; estate account opened; notice to creditors published.	Order for Probate; Letters Testamentary.
4	Inventory completed and filed; appraisal of real estate; first creditor claims received.	Inventory filed.
5	Decedent's final 1040 filed (if year-end has passed); creditor evaluation continues.	—
6	Creditor-claim window closes (varies by state); claims paid or rejected.	—
7	Estate-tax planning, basis allocation, partial distributions where authorized.	—
8	Estate income-tax return (Form 1041) prepared; investment management ongoing.	—
9	Federal estate-tax return (Form 706) due (if applicable); state estate-tax filings.	Form 706 filed if required.
10	Final accounting prepared; petition for distribution drafted.	—

Month	Principal activities	Court touch points
11	Petition for distribution filed; notice to beneficiaries; objection window.	Petition filed; hearing scheduled.
12	Hearing on petition; order approving accounting; distributions made; receipts collected.	Order for Final Distribution; Order Discharging Executor.

Twelve-month estate administration calendar (typical, uncontested).

An estate that closes by the end of the twelfth month is a well-administered estate. An estate that closes by the end of the ninth month — uncommon but possible — is an extraordinary one.

APPENDIX H

The Family Communication Framework

We have argued in Chapter 9 that the single most effective tool for preventing intra-family conflict during probate is regular, written communication from the executor to the beneficiaries. This appendix provides a framework.

The Monthly Update

Once a month, on the same day each month, the executor sends a brief written update to all beneficiaries. The update has the same five sections each month:

1. **Status of the administration.** Where we are in the process — the creditor window, the inventory, the tax return. One paragraph.
2. **What was completed in the past month.** Petition filed, inventory completed, Form 706 filed. Bullet list.
3. **What is happening this month.** What the executor is working on now. Bullet list.
4. **What is next.** The next milestone and the expected timing. One paragraph.

5. **Anything the beneficiaries need to know.** Tax forms they will receive, requests for information, decisions they may want to consider. Plain language.

The update should be no longer than one page. It should be sent to all beneficiaries simultaneously, with each as a named recipient — not as a forwarded message. The same update should not vary between branches of the family. Consistency is the entire point.

When Something Difficult Must Be Communicated

When the executor must communicate news that some or all beneficiaries will dislike — a will provision being clearly applied in a way one branch hoped to avoid, a creditor claim that will reduce distributions, the rejection of a beneficiary's request — the cleanest approach is:

1. **State the news directly.** Without preamble. Without softening that disguises the substance. Beneficiaries respect direct communication; they resent communication that requires them to read between lines.

2. **Explain the procedural reason.** Why the will, the statute, or the creditor claim controls. Reference the relevant document or rule.

3. **Acknowledge the impact.** Without arguing about whether the impact is fair. The impact is real. Saying so does not concede anything.

4. **Identify the next step.** What happens next, when, and what the beneficiary's options are.
5. **Offer to discuss.** By phone or in person. Some beneficiaries will accept; most will not. The offer matters either way.

Executors who communicate difficult news this way close estates with the family substantially intact. Executors who try to manage the communication — softening, deflecting, hiding behind counsel — discover that the beneficiaries' anxiety transfers to the next decision and accumulates.

APPENDIX I

Subject Index

The following index lists principal terms and concepts treated in this volume, alphabetically, with the chapter (and where useful, the table or figure) where each is treated. Page-precise references are available in the printed edition.

APPENDIX J

A Reader's Quick-Start Guide

If you have come to this book because someone has just died and you need to act, this appendix is a single-page distillation of the most important early steps. It is not a substitute for the full chapters, but it will get you oriented in the first week.

What to Do First

1. **Order ten to fifteen original death certificates.** From the funeral home or the vital-records office.
2. **Find the will.** Check the safe, the safe-deposit box, the attorney's office, the filing cabinet. Look for the original — not a copy.
3. **Secure the residence.** Locks. Mail. Pets. Perishables. Vehicles.
4. **Engage probate counsel.** A first meeting at low or no cost. Most counsel will help even before the petition is filed.
5. **Do not distribute personal property yet.** Even when the family agrees, premature distribution complicates the inventory and creates dispute risk.

What Will Take Time

- The court's first hearing — typically four to eight weeks out.
- Letters Testamentary — typically six to ten weeks out.
- The creditor-claim window — three to seven months from publication.
- Tax-return cycles — four to nine months for ordinary cases.
- Final distribution — typically months ten through fourteen.

What to Avoid

- Promising distributions to family members on a calendar you cannot meet.
- Negotiating with creditors before counsel is engaged.
- Selling property before authority is in hand.
- Acting on advice from television or a single internet thread.
- Treating the executor's role as informal.

What to Read in This Book First

Chapter 3 (the first thirty days), Chapter 4 (the executor's role), Appendix C (the first-sixty-days checklist), and Appendix G (the twelve-month calendar). Those four sections together cover roughly ninety percent of what you need to know in your first week.

APPENDIX K

Notes on The Complete Estate & Property Planning Series

The Complete Estate & Property Planning Series is AVOY Publishing's flagship project — a four-book institutional reference that treats, taken together, the four pillars of American post-mortem asset transfer. The series is written for the intelligent reader who is tired of being talked down to. Each volume is designed to be read on its own. The four volumes also cross-reference one another for readers who wish to build a broader picture.

The Four Books in the Series

The series is organized around the four mechanisms by which American families transfer wealth at and after death — and the four matters every family should understand before the transfer occurs.

1. **Book 1 — Trust Made Simple.** The foundational treatment of the trust as instrument: revocable and irrevocable, intra-vivos and testamentary, with extended treatment of the trust-funding discipline that determines whether a plan actually works at death.

2. **Book 2 — Probate Explained (this volume).** The institutional-grade explanation of probate itself: what it is, when it happens, who runs it, why it takes the time it takes, where families get stuck, and how it ends. The starting point for any reader who has just lost someone or is preparing for what comes.
3. **Book 3 — Property After Death.** Real property — houses, land, vacation homes, farms, fractional interests — is the asset Americans most often own, most often misunderstand, and most often litigate. Book 3 treats how property moves at and after death in the same plain-language style as the rest of the series.
4. **Book 4 — Estate Taxes Explained.** The capstone volume — the federal and state transfer-tax regime explained for the family that has the assets to be exposed to it but no specialist on retainer. Estate tax, gift tax, generation-skipping transfer tax, basis step-up rules, and the planning architecture that minimizes the tax and preserves the wealth.

Reading the Series Together

The four volumes share a deliberate architecture. Trust Made Simple establishes the principal probate-avoidance vehicle. Probate Explained (this volume) treats the alternative — the court-supervised transfer that occurs when no trust applies. Property After Death drills into the asset category that produces the most family pain regardless of which path applies. Estate Taxes Explained treats the tax overlay that shapes the entire structure for substantial estates.

Read in order, the series gives you a complete mental model of post-mortem asset transfer in American private law. Read individually — each volume stands alone — and you will still have a definitive treatment of the subject the title names.

Future Editions and Notification

AVOY Publishing intends to maintain each volume in the series with periodic editions reflecting changes in tax law, state statutes, and practice. Readers who would like to receive notice of future editions, supplementary materials, or additional volumes can request to be added to the series notification list at ap@avoyhq.com.

APPENDIX L

Chapter-by-Chapter Summary

This summary is intended for readers who have completed the book and want a single page that captures the principal idea of each chapter. It is also useful for readers returning to the book years later and looking for a particular treatment without re-reading the full text.

Chapter 1 — What Probate Is (and Why It Exists)

Probate is the system that creates legal authority to act for an estate when the owner is no longer here. It exists for the orderly transfer of title, the protection of creditors, and the enforcement of testamentary intent. It is not about families.

Chapter 2 — When Probate Happens (and When It Doesn't)

Probate is triggered when individually titled assets exist at death. It is avoided by funded trusts, joint titling, and beneficiary designations. Two estates with identical balance sheets can have entirely different probate experiences depending on how assets were structured before death.

Chapter 3 — The First 30 Days After Death

The first month is mostly waiting. Letters Testamentary do not issue until the court has held the first hearing, typically six to ten weeks after death. The wait is the system functioning, not failing.

Chapter 4 — The Role of the Executor

The executor is a court-recognized administrator with fiduciary duty. The role is wide and detailed but follows a knowable sequence. Compensation, liability, and family tension are the three principal considerations.

Chapter 5 — What the Court Actually Does

The probate court does five things: confirms authority, polices the procedure, resolves disputes, approves significant transactions, and approves the closing. Everything else happens between those touch points.

Chapter 6 — Why Probate Takes So Long

Probate duration is driven by four largely fixed inputs (notice, creditor window, tax filings, court calendar) and one variable input (estate complexity). Eight to twelve months is typical for uncontested estates of ordinary complexity.

Chapter 7 — What Causes Delays and Disputes

Six recurring sources of delay (missing documents, unclear ownership, beneficiary disagreement, contested debts, hard-to-value assets, tax complications) and three categories of dispute (will contests, fiduciary disputes, distribution disputes) account for nearly every case that takes longer than it should.

Chapter 8 — What Families Get Wrong About Probate

Ten common misunderstandings — including the belief that the will avoids probate, that the executor controls everything, and that probate costs half the estate — produce most avoidable family conflict. Correcting them is the work of any honest estate-planning conversation.

Chapter 9 — Why Probate Feels Personal

Probate happens during grief. The legal calendar and the emotional calendar do not align. Communication — regular, written, consistent — is the single most effective tool for preventing avoidable intra-family conflict.

Chapter 10 — What Happens When Probate Ends

Probate ends quietly: a final accounting, an order of distribution, an order discharging the executor. The estate as a legal entity ceases to exist. Some obligations survive (testamentary trusts, tax matters, narrow categories of subsequent claim). The institution has done what it was designed to do.

Chapter 11 — When Probate Meets a Trust

Most modern estates pass through some combination of trust, pour-over will, beneficiary designations, and joint titling. The pour-over will is the safety net; the trust is the principal vehicle. The single most common failure is the funding gap — assets the settlor failed to retitle during life. Lifetime funding discipline is what makes the rest of the plan work as designed.

Chapter 12 — Special Situations: When Probate Becomes Unusual

Six categories of special situation account for most non-textbook probate cases: blended families, multi-state real property, minor beneficiaries, beneficiaries with disabilities, digital assets, and missing-original-will cases. Each is anticipatable with appropriate drafting; together, they account for a meaningful share of the cases practitioners describe as difficult.

APPENDIX M

Creditor-Claim Priority Order

When an estate's debts exceed its assets, the order in which valid claims are paid is determined by statute. The order is largely consistent across states, although terminology and specific categories vary. This appendix presents the priority order in the form most states follow.

Table M.1

Priority	Class	Examples
1	Costs of administration	Court fees, executor compensation, attorney fees, accountant fees, appraisal fees.
2	Funeral and burial expenses	Reasonable funeral, burial, and last-illness expenses.
3	Family allowance	Statutory support payments to surviving spouse and minor children during administration.
4	Debts and taxes due to government	Federal and state taxes, including income, estate, and inheritance taxes.
5	Secured claims	Claims secured by liens on estate property (mortgages, perfected security interests).
6	Last illness expenses	Reasonable medical expenses of the deceased's last illness, where not already paid.
7	Wages owed	Wages and salary owed to employees of the deceased for limited periods preceding death.
8	General unsecured claims	Credit-card balances, ordinary trade debt, judgments not previously secured.
9	Subrogated and contingent claims	Claims by guarantors or sureties subrogated to creditors.

Typical priority order for payment of claims against a probate estate.

Lower-priority creditors receive nothing if higher-priority claims exhaust the estate. Within a priority class, claims are generally paid pro rata if class assets are insufficient. Secured claims may be satisfied from the security regardless of priority, with any deficiency reduced to a general claim of corresponding rank.

Executors administering an insolvent estate must follow the priority order strictly. Paying a lower-priority creditor before a higher one — even unintentionally, even out of sympathy — exposes the executor personally to the higher-priority creditor's claim. This is one of the categories where the procedure looks harsh and is, in fact, exactly what protects the executor and the estate from preference litigation.

APPENDIX N

Ancillary Probate — When Real Property Crosses State Lines

Ancillary probate is the proceeding required when a deceased person owned real property in a state other than their state of domicile. This appendix explains what triggers ancillary probate, how it works, and how to manage the additional administrative burden it produces.

What Triggers Ancillary Probate

Real property is governed by the law of the state in which it is located, regardless of where the owner lived. When a Florida resident dies owning a vacation home in North Carolina, the Florida probate (the principal probate) administers everything except that vacation home. North Carolina law — specifically, North Carolina probate procedure — administers the vacation home in a separate ancillary proceeding.

The trigger is the location of real property. Personal property (brokerage accounts, bank accounts, vehicles registered in the domicile state) is governed by the law of the domicile, not by where the property is physically located. Only real property — land and the buildings on it — produces an ancillary requirement.

How Ancillary Probate Works

The principal probate proceeds normally in the deceased's home state. After Letters Testamentary issue in the home state, the executor (or local counsel retained in the ancillary state) files a separate petition in the second state, typically asking the second state's court to recognize the home-state appointment and admit the will to ancillary probate. Most states have a streamlined procedure for this — sometimes called domiciliary ancillary or foreign probate — that reduces but does not eliminate the second proceeding.

The ancillary court then issues its own Letters or its own order of appointment, which authorizes the executor to act with respect to the real property in that state. The ancillary proceeding has its own creditor-claim window, its own inventory (of the ancillary property only), and its own closing requirements.

How to Avoid Ancillary Probate

The cleanest way to avoid ancillary probate is to title the out-of-state real property in a way that does not require probate. Common approaches:

- Title the property in a revocable trust during life. The trust holds the property; no probate of any kind is required at death.

- Title the property jointly with right of survivorship between spouses, where appropriate. The survivor takes by operation of law.
- Use a transfer-on-death (Lady-Bird) deed in states that recognize them. The recorded deed transfers the property automatically at death without a probate proceeding.
- Hold the property through a single-member LLC owned by a trust, where the use justifies the ongoing entity costs.

The choice depends on the use of the property, the family's tax circumstances, and the second state's specific recognition of particular instruments. The most important moment to make this decision is when the out-of-state property is acquired, not at the eventual death — though it is rarely too late to retitle.

Estimated Time and Cost

An ancillary probate adds, on average, four to nine months to the principal administration. Cost varies, but ten to twenty thousand dollars in additional fees and costs is a typical range for an uncontested ancillary involving a single residential property. More complex cases — multiple parcels, contested title, out-of-state business interests — can add substantially to both the calendar and the cost.

The economics of avoiding ancillary probate, in other words, almost always favor the planning. A two-thousand-dollar deed filing during life saves a fifteen-thousand-dollar proceeding after death.

A FINAL WORD

On Legacy, Care, and the Quiet Years Before

◆

You have come to the end of this volume. You have read, perhaps, more about probate than you ever expected to need to know.

And yet what this book has been describing, in its own structured way, is something quieter and larger than probate itself.

It has been describing the act of taking care.

The institution of probate exists because someone, at some point in the long history of private law, decided that the property of a person who is no longer here should reach the people that person loved — lawfully, fairly, and without the chaos of unstructured grief. Every will ever drafted, every trust ever funded, every beneficiary designation ever signed, is at its root the same act: someone before us deciding that they wanted the people they loved to be cared for after they were gone.

That act of care is what survives all of us. It survives our names. It survives the houses we owned and the accounts we kept and the businesses we built. It is the part of us that gets handed forward.

You have learned what probate is, when it happens, who runs it, why it takes its time, where families get stuck, and how it ends. What you do now with that knowledge — for yourself, for your family, for the people who will eventually administer what you leave behind — is the real subject of this book.

Sit down with the people you love. Have the conversation you have been postponing. Sign the documents that make your wishes legible. Update them once a year. Tell your successor where the originals are. Live the rest of your life with the quiet knowledge that the structure is in place.

That is the legacy worth building. Everything else — the probate calendar, the executor's duties, the appendices and forms and timelines we have spent these pages laying out — is in service of it.

"A plan is not made in the moment of crisis. It is made in the quiet years before the crisis, and tested — silently, invisibly — every day thereafter. The legacy worth leaving is the one your loved ones never have to wonder about."

Take care of yours.

— AVOY Publishing

Spring 2026

Made in United States
Cleveland, OH
08 November 2026

47789691R00148